Abnormal Psychology

FOUNDATIONS OF MODERN PSYCHOLOGY SERIES
*Richard S. Lazarus, Editor*

**SHELDON CASHDAN**

Associate Professor of Psychology
University of Massachusetts

# Abnormal Psychology

PRENTICE-HALL, INC., ENGLEWOOD CLIFFS, NEW JERSEY

© 1972 by
Prentice-Hall, Inc., Englewood Cliffs, N.J.

ISBN: P-O-13-000794-3;  C-O-13-000802-8

Current printing (last digit)
10 9 8 7 6 5 4 3 2 1

Prentice-Hall International, Inc., London

Prentice-Hall of Australia, Pty. Ltd., Sydney

Prentice-Hall of Canada, Ltd., Toronto

Prentice-Hall of India Priviate Limited, New Delhi

Prentice-Hall of Japan, Inc., Tokyo

*For Eva*

# Contents

# Foundations of
# Modern Psychology Series

The tremendous growth and vitality of psychology and its increasing fusion with the social and biological sciences demand a search for new approaches to teaching at the introductory level. We can no longer feel content with the traditional basic course, geared as it usually is to a single text that tries to skim everything, that sacrifices depth for breadth. Psychology has become too diverse for any one man, or few men, to write about with complete authority. The alternative, a book that ignores many essential areas in order to present more comprehensively and effectively a particular aspect or view of psychology, is also insufficient, for in this solution many key areas are simply not communicated to the student at all.

The Foundations of Modern Psychology Series was the first in what has become a growing trend in psychology toward groups of short texts dealing with various basic subjects, each written by an active authority. It was conceived with the idea of providing greater flexibility for instructors teaching general courses than was ordinarily available in the large, encyclopedic textbooks, and greater depth of presentation for individual topics not typically given much space in introductory textbooks.

The earliest volumes appeared in 1963, the latest not until 1972. Well over one and a quarter million copies, collectively, have been sold, attesting to the widespread use of these books in the teaching of psychology. Individual volumes have been used as supplementary texts, or as *the* text, in various undergraduate courses in psychology, education, public health, and sociology, and clusters of volumes have served as the text in beginning undergraduate courses in general psychology. Groups of volumes have been translated into eight languages, including Dutch, Hebrew, Italian, Japanese, Polish, Portuguese, Spanish, and Swedish.

With wide variation in publication date and type of content, some of the volumes need revision, while others do not. We have left this decision to the individual author who best knows his book in relation to the state of the field. Some will remain unchanged, some will be modestly changed, and still others completely rewritten. In the new series edition, we have also opted for some variation in the length and style of individual books, to reflect the different ways in which they have been used as texts.

There has never been stronger interest in good teaching in our colleges and universities than there is now; and for this the availability of high quality, well-written, and stimulating text materials highlighting the exciting and continuing search for knowledge is a prime prerequisite. This is especially the case in undergraduate courses where large numbers of students must have access to suitable readings. The Foundations of Modern Psychology Series represents our ongoing attempt to provide college teachers with the best textbook materials we can create.

# Preface

The world of abnormal psychology is intriguing, mysterious, challenging and, most of all, complex. Its complexity derives not only from the nature of its subject matter—disordered human behavior—but from the fact that it can be approached from a number of different perspectives. The subjective impressions of the mental patient, the empirical findings of the researcher, and the clinical experience of the psychotherapist all yield unique insights into the nature of pathological phenomena.

This introductory text focuses on topics that best convey what each perspective has to offer. To provide the beginning student with a means of ordering the diverse material in the field, topics are discussed within the context of changing models of psychopathology. My hope is to convey an appreciation for the different ways in which abnormal behavior can be understood as well as to provide the student with a conceptual stepping-stone for future study.

I wish to take this opportunity to express my appreciation to Seymour Epstein and Norman Watt for reading portions of the manuscript and making valuable suggestions. Thanks also are due Rinda Iascone and Betty Cinq-Mars who freely gave of their time in the technical preparation of the manuscript. I am especially indebted to the editor of this series, Richard Lazarus. Through a deft blend of warm encouragement and critical advice, he always was able to convince me that I could do better when I was convinced I had done my best.

Sheldon Cashdan

# Acknowledgements

For permission to quote from: Joseph Church, *Language and the Discovery of Reality,* © 1961 by Random House, Inc.; F. Peters, *The World Next Door,* © 1949 by Arthur A. Peters, reprinted by permission of Russell & Volkening, Inc.; Jay Haley, *Strategies of Psychotherapy,* by permission of Grune & Stratton, Inc.; H. Mullan and M. Rosenbaum, *Group Psychotherapy,* © 1962 by The Macmillan Company; Milton Rokeach, *The Three Christs of Ypsilanti,* © 1964 by Alfred A. Knopf, Inc.; Ronald Sullivan, "Violence, Like Charity, Begins at Home," © 1968 by The New York Times Company, reprinted by permission; Paul Watzlawick, Janet Helmick Beavin, and Don D. Jackson, *Pragmatics of Human Communication,* reprinted by permission of W.W. Norton & Company, Inc., © 1967 by W.W. Norton & Company, Inc.; L.R. Wolberg, *The Technique of Psychotherapy,* by permission of Grune & Stratton, Inc.; M. Zax and G. Stricker, *Patterns of Psychopathology,* © 1963 by The Macmillan Company. Fig. 2 of the book is reprinted from the *Encyclopedia of Witchcraft and Demonology* by Russell Hope Robbins, © 1959 by Crown Publishers, Inc., used with the permission of Crown Publishers, Inc.; Figs. 5 and 6, reprinted from Harris in the *Journal of Personality,* vol. 25 (1957), © 1957 by the Duke University Press; Fig. 16, © 1968 by United Features Syndicate, Inc.

Abnormal Psychology

# Models of Abnormal Behavior

## chapter one

"Hate and disgust is what I feel for myself." With these words, Charles M. began psychotherapy. A successful, forty-five-year-old senior architect in a large building firm, he was seeking help for a disabling fear of heights that in recent months had begun to seriously interfere with his work. Although Mr. M. had in the past been able to minimize his anxiety by avoiding heights, he was beginning to find this more difficult. His firm had recently contracted to build a series of large apartment buildings and asked him to supervise the construction. This requires him to conduct periodic inspections, a task that includes traveling to upper stories by open elevator. Just the thought of this results in shortness of breath, cold sweats, and feelings of panic. In attempting to avoid this assignment, Mr. M. concocted a number of complicated excuses, and even called in ill on several occasions in order to avoid conducting inspections. Unable to understand the basis for his problem and ashamed of having to continually deceive his associates, he entered therapy hoping somehow to find a solution to his predicament.

Neil C., the son of a wealthy businessman, is an attractive teenager who is quite popular among his peers. A senior in high school, he has his own car and receives a generous allowance. Nevertheless, in recent months, Neil has stolen two automobiles and forged numerous checks. The cars were abandoned soon after they were taken and the money from the checks merely frittered away. In several of these instances, Neil was apprehended by authorities but was rescued from a possible jail sentence by his father's influence. A brief survey of Neil's past reveals a series of dangerous and senseless escapades. On two occasions he was involved in high-speed automobile chases after refusing to stop for minor traffic violations. On another occasion he came close to being shot. This occurred when he jokingly tossed some firecrackers under a Brinks armored truck and found himself suddenly confronted by guards bearing drawn weapons. Despite the outcome of his escapades, Neil always returns to the same pattern, relatively unaffected by his experiences.

Mary L., a college sophomore first treated at a Student Mental Health Service, traced her difficulties to her freshman year. Soon after entering college, she found herself becoming very anxious without being able to identify the cause. In addition, she often experienced a vague feeling that things were not quite right. Her plans always seemed to fall apart and she suspected that people were gossiping about her. Mary nonetheless could not quite put her finger on precisely what was going on. In her sophomore year, Mary's strange experiences suddenly began to make sense. All the pieces fell into place as she realized that a small group of powerful professors, called "The Council," was secretly using her as a guinea pig in an important experiment. Mary was convinced that these professors not only had hand-picked her courses, but made them especially difficult in order to test her endurance and intelligence. In line with their overall plan, her exam performances were carefully scrutinized and subsequent exams made more difficult. Mary was also sure that her room in the dorm was bugged and that hidden, closed-circuit TV cameras were monitoring her every move. While Mary at first felt put upon, she later attempted to please the council by desperately trying to live up to its standards. She soon became very fatigued, her schoolwork began to suffer, and she was ultimately referred to the Mental Health Service by her dorm counselor.

The behavior described in these case studies, while perplexing and occasionally bizzare, is not uncommon. Practically everyone knows of a friend or relative who has been treated by a psychologist or psychiatrist; most of us know someone who has spent time in a mental hospital. The widespread use of the phrase "nervous breakdown" reflects the prevalence of mental illness in our society.

But mental illness is not unique to our culture nor to our time. It has been with us for thousands of years and has been received in many different ways. In the course of history, people who behaved abnormally were, at one time or another, isolated, tortured, and sometimes killed; their behavior was viewed not as mental illness but as immorality, heresy, and witchcraft. Today we speak instead of "mental disturbances" and "emotional disorders," and think of the afflicted as unfortunate human beings to be treated and helped rather than tortured and ridiculed. Our current views of psychopathology seem to be more humane and sophisticated than those of the past.

But are they? Exactly how is mental illness viewed today? How does the public construe the bizzare and often frightening phenomena that fall into the category of abnormal behavior? A cursory examination indicates that even though most people know or have heard of someone who has had a "breakdown," very few can claim extensive contact with the mentally ill. The public's view of mental illness must therefore derive from something other than personal experience, and close analysis suggests that our current views, both positive and negative, are rooted in a complex combination of fact and folk myth. Therefore in order to better understand our current conceptions of mental disturbances, we must turn to the history of abnormal psychology.

At every point in history professionals and laymen have tried to make sense of strange and puzzling behavior. Inevitably this has resulted in attempts to label such behavior, uncover its cause, and treat it. When taken together, these ideas on identification, causation, and treatment constitute a *model* of abnormal behavior. Our trip into the past focuses on these models with particular attention to the ways in which they have changed throughout the years. In the process, we will show how different models evolve and how each one generates its own unique approach to psychotherapy.

## Demonological vs. Naturalistic Models

The demonological model of deviant behavior is based on the belief that mystical agents are capable of significantly influencing human behavior. Benevolent spirits are thought to underlie positive actions; evil spirits are responsible for negative occurrences. The belief that strange behavior must be the result of unknown powerful forces probably represents mankind's first attempt to explain physical and mental disease.

The naturalistic model, in contrast, places the source of deviant behavior within the body in naturally occurring physical processes. Abnormal behavior, according to this model, is related to abnormal body functions. The naturalistic model thus is the direct antithesis of the demonological doctrine. In the following pages we will illustrate how mankind's initial attempts to understand abnormal behavior were related in part to the ways in which these two models vied for dominance.

ANCIENT VIEWS

In the early days of man, human beings not only failed to distinguish between physical and mental disorders, but had little conception of the body's biological makeup. In prehistoric times the human body was probably viewed as a homogeneous entity in much the same way that we view the amoeba today. Since primitive man was ignorant of his own anatomy and physiology, he could not explain strange behavior on the basis of natural factors, and instead attributed it to foreign agents or spirits that somehow were able to enter the body.

Evidence exists to suggest that Stone Age man not only believed in evil spirits but also tried to do something to remove them. Crudely bored holes indicative of an operation called *trephining* have been noted in the skulls of prehistoric man. Trephining was apparently designed to allow the evil spirits trapped within a person to escape, and constitutes one of

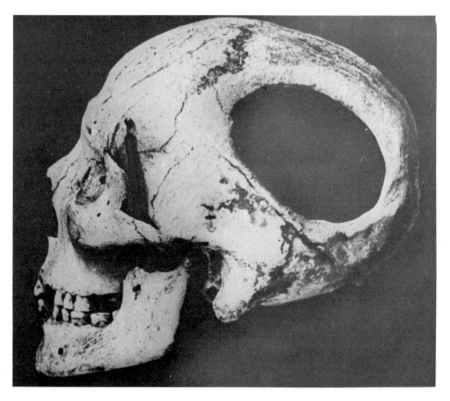

FIGURE 1.　Archaeological evidence of trephining. (Bettman Archive).

man's early attempts to treat mental illness. This crude form of brain surgery was the historical precursor of the psychosurgical techniques that would be used to treat the mentally ill in the twentieth century.

The advent of the Hebrew and early Greek civilizations saw little appreciable advance in man's conception of abnormal behavior. The Bible contains numerous references to behaviors that we recognize today as signs of personality disturbance, but then were seen as signs of mystical influence. Saul, for example, suffered from depression and homicidal impulses, disorders thought to be caused by evil spirits sent by God. Leviticus contains the foreboding statement: "A man also or woman that hath a familiar spirit, or that is a wizard, shall surely be put to death" (Leviticus 20:27). This last pronouncement reflects the aura of superstition and fear surrounding the mentally ill in biblical days, and later provided the rationale for the witchburnings of the Middle Ages.

It should not be surprising to learn that those who behaved abnormally were left to wander the countryside or imprisoned in dungeons; the superstitions and fears of any culture are invariably reflected in the open rejection and active persecution of those it cannot understand. Nevertheless, there were at least some attempts to understand and treat the mentally ill. In ancient Greece, Aesculapian temples, named after the Greek god of healing, grew into centers of medicine and provided havens for disturbed persons. Within these temples, priestlike physicians prescribed rest and potions and acted as interpreters of dreams. Services such as these, however, were reserved for the elite; those who could not afford the cure continued to be treated in dismal ways.

As countless physicians, prophets, and priests were called upon to explain abnormal behavior, the demonological model became increasingly refined. Some of the mentally ill were thought to possess curative powers of their own and were subsequently allowed to treat others. Demonological theorists also began to make fine distinctions between malevolent and benevolent types of disorders. Epilepsy, for example, was thought to have favorable mystical significance; it was referred to as the "sacred disease" and for hundreds of years was thought to be a sign of divine favor.

In approximately 400 b.c., this morass of superstition and confusion was suddenly challenged by Hippocrates, the father of medicine. Writing about epilepsy he stated:

It thus appears to me to be in no way more divine, nor more sacred than other diseases, but has a natural cause from which it originates like other affections. If you cut open the head, you will find the brain humid, full of sweat, and smelling badly. And in this way you may see that it is not a god which injures the body, but disease.

By placing the source of abnormal behavior within the body's physical processes, Hippocrates almost singlehandedly removed it from the province of demonology. The doctrine of *naturalism* now emerged as a potent alternative to the demonological model of mental illness. The origin of deviant behavior was placed within natural body processes rather than in spiritual phenomena.

Hippocrates also contributed to the development of abnormal psychology by distinguishing among epilepsy, states of extreme excitement (mania), and states of extreme depression which he labeled melancholia (Zilboorg and Henry, 1941). Many view the distinctions he drew as the first *nosology*, or classification system, in the field of abnormal psychology. It should be recognized, however, that his specific ideas about causation were not as advanced as his classifications. Hippocrates felt that all illnesses were caused by an excess of *humors*—hypothetical fluids that were thought to circulate within the body.

Hippocrates' radical ideas were further advanced by a great Roman physician named Galen who lived between 100 and 200 A.D. Like Hippocrates, Galen supported the idea that disturbances in the humoral system caused most of man's ailments, and his refinements of the theory of humors were so erudite they prevailed for over a thousand years. Although it was eventually discarded, humor theory tended to support the naturalistic model of mental illness by placing the cause of all human dysfunction within the body.

The death of Galen in 200 A.D., coupled with the spread of Christianity, signalled a dramatic turnabout. As the Church became a more powerful political and social instrument, it eventually displaced the physician as the guardian of the human body and soul. The naturalistic model of mental illness was soon to be abandoned.

MEDIEVAL VIEWS

The doctrine of demonology, nourished within the protective cloak of Church dogma, once again began to bloom. Care of the mentally ill was placed in the hands of priests and monks, and medical treatment replaced by prayer and penance. Abnormal behavior was now explained as the work of the devil. By the fifth century, magic was officially condemned as heresy and the task of the Church became increasingly clearcut—secure man's liberation from the invisible forces of Satan. From within the Church emerged demonologists whose job it was to identify possessed individuals and free them from the devil's influence.

In the early part of the Middle Ages, attempts at driving out, or exorcising, demons were relatively mild. For the most part, they involved persuading the possessed individual to touch religious relics, say prayers, and take magical potions. Directions for preparing one magical potion thought to be extremely effective reads:

> Take a testicle of a goat that has been killed on a Tuesday midnight, during the first quarter of the moon, and the heart of a dog, mix with the excrement of a newborn babe, and after pulverizing, take an amount equivalent to half an olive twice a day. (Roback, 1961, p. 215)

As the Middle Ages progressed and the doctrine of demonology became more refined, the writings of demonologists began to include more detailed descriptions of how to detect the devil's presence. The occurrence of visions, which today we would label visual hallucinations, were commonly considered indications of possession, as were *stigmata diaboli* (signs of the devil). Stigmata included such things as moles and pigmented areas as of the skin, as well as skin anesthesias, areas on the skin which yielded little or no sensation. Skin anesthesias are today regarded as symptoms of neurosis if they cannot be explained neurologically.

Toward the end of the medieval period, demonologists traveled with assistants called *prickers* who carried special knife-like instruments to probe the bodies of suspected persons for insensitive areas. Since prickers were paid for every correct identification, they were not above using trickery; the blades of some of their instruments could secretly be withdrawn into a hollow handle so that when pressed against the body of an accused, it would cause no pain (see Fig. 2, p. 8). This sign of skin anesthesia then provided conclusive evidence of demoniacal possession.

The advent of the Inquisition toward the end of the Middle Ages led to the wholesale use of brutal punishment for dissenters. Inquisitors trained in every conceivable form of torture traveled throughout Europe searching out and persecuting innumerable innocent souls in the name of God and the Church. Although a few courageous voices were raised in opposition, they were drowned out by the mass hysteria of the day. By the fifteenth century, the concepts of mental illness, heresy, and witchcraft were firmly fused, and the stage was set for the appearance of the infamous witch-hunting manual, *Malleus Maleficarum* ("Hammer of the Witches").

In 1484, two Dominican monks named Johann Sprenger and Heinrich Kraemer received Papal authority to write an authoritative guide of demonology and witchcraft. Sprenger and Kraemer wisely consolidated their position by also obtaining a stamp of approval from the Theology Faculty at the University of Cologne. Armed with the impressive credentials of the Church and the University, they published the *Malleus Maleficarum* and set out to spread the teachings contained within it.

The *Malleus* was made up of three parts. The first attempted to verify

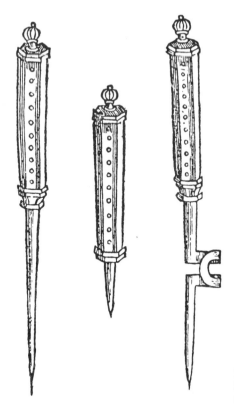

FIGURE 2. Examples of pricking instruments. From *The Encyclopedia of Witchcraft and Demonology* (Robbins, 1959).

the existence of witches and argued the need for trained administrators to conduct inquisitions; the second presented detailed accounts of the evil witches do and how to detect their presence; the last part provided formal procedures for bringing a witch to trial and for sentencing her. Almost without fail, conviction meant the accused was either strangled to death or burned at the stake.

But a witch could not be executed, no matter how strong the evidence, unless a confession was obtained. Part three of the *Malleus* conveniently offered specific techniques for obtaining confessions from the accused. These techniques invariably culminated in some form of torture, and were spelled out in excruciating detail. A common method of forcing confessions was called strappado (from the Latin *strappeare*, to pull).

> The prisoner's arms were tied behind his back with a rope attached to a pulley, and he was then hoisted in the air. Frequently, weights were attached to his feet to pull his shoulders from their sockets without leaving visible marks of rough treatment. (Robbins, 1959, p. 489)

As incredible as it may seem, this was not considered a particularly drastic form of torture. *The Encyclopedia of Witchcraft and Demonology* (1959) states, "Strappado was customarily one of the 'lighter' measures used by the Inquisition and the civil authorities, but could easily develop into squassation, a more severe variant (p. 489)." The exaggerated misconceptions of the mentally ill that today we label delusions were then taken as confessions of demonological possession and provided the rationale for the use of torture and execution.

The perversity of the *Malleus Maleficarum* is accentuated by its open unmitigated hatred of women. It is estimated that for every man convicted as a sorcerer, fifty women were burned at the stake. The rationale for this was terrifyingly simple: Women were weak, tainted creatures who were more likely than men to succumb to the devil's influence. By and large, this influence was transmitted by sexual means; women were transformed into witches through intercourse with the devil. The devil also spread his evil indirectly by loosing lustful sexual demons called *incubi* on unsuspecting women. Incubi had their counterparts in *succubi*, or female demons, but they were reported less frequently. Frigidity, im-

FIGURE 3. Early woodcut of a devil making love to a woman. From *De Lamiis* (1489) by a Ulrich Molitor, courtesy of the Cornell University Library.

potence, lechery, and other forms of sexual deviance thus came to be attributed to the devil and his emissaries. Mental illness and sexual sin became inseparable. The sexual problems that today are tied to guilt, fear, and misinformation were viewed in medieval times as signs of demonic possession.

In the hands of the Christian inquisitors, the *Malleus Maleficarum* functioned as a crude but effective means of suppressing many forms of deviance in medieval Europe, much of which today would be categorized as "mental illness." Zilboorg and Henry (1941) point to the social and political restlessness of the time and suggest that the *Malleus* was a "reaction against the disquieting signs of growing instability of the established order (p. 153)." Even though the mentally ill were not particularly anti-establishment, they were the most visible class of deviants, and hundreds of thousands were systematically exterminated.

At the same time witches were being burned in the sixteenth century, voices once again were being raised against the doctrine of demonology. The strongest belonged to a German physician named Johann Weyer. Weyer challenged the entire structure of theological demonism by writing a two-volume text directly contradicting the *Malleus Maleficarum*. This event marked one of the beginnings of an enlightened view toward abnormal behavior.

*De Praestigiis Daemonum* ("On Demonological Magic"), Weyer's major work published in 1563, is a point-by-point dissection of the *Malleus*. It first carefully undermines Sprenger's and Kraemer's superstitious contentions by methodically examining their illogical assumptions. Secondly, it contains Weyer's own explanation for bizarre behavior and provides anecdotal evidence to substantiate his claims. Finally, it chastises the sadistic priests for their inhumane practices, reminding them that it is their duty to cure rather than to kill.

The writings of Johann Weyer constitute one of the significant factors in the demise of demonology, and were a major reason for the resurrection of the naturalistic model. Nevertheless, strong, ingrained beliefs did not perish easily. As much as two hundred years after the publication of *De Praestigiis*, two witches were decapitated in central Europe, one in Germany and one in Switzerland.

Is a supernatural view of human behavior still subscribed to? Judging by the renewed interest in witchcraft, astrology, and Eastern mystical thought, the answer would probably have to be yes, although most people do not *really* believe in demons and witches that enter the human body to do evil. Or do they? Perhaps it is only a quirk of English usage that leads us to respond to individuals who behave strangely with, "I wonder what's gotten *into* him!"

## MEDICAL AND SOCIAL REFORMS

Although demonology and witchburning were fading by the middle 1700's, the mentally ill were still harshly treated. Many were kept in jails and almshouses, while thousands more wandered the streets begging for food. In addition, the mental hospitals of the time were no more than large prisons. In England, the inmates of Bethlehem Hospital (referred to then as Bedlam) were handcuffed and chained to the walls. Patients were sometimes put on display for the amusement of Londoners who were not averse to paying a small fee to see a lunatic sideshow. Treatment for the most part did not exist, and mental patients were fortunate if they just could manage to avoid the punishment of sadistic jailers.

The situation was not much different in France. Patients in French asylums were also treated like wild animals. A French physician named Esquirol, after inspecting these asylums, wrote:

> I have seen them naked, or covered with rags, and protected only by straw from the cold damp pavement. . . . I have seen them in squalid stinking little hovels, without air or light, chained in caves where wild beasts would not have been confined. . . . There they remain to waste away in their own filth under the weight of chains which lacerate their bodies. . . . Whips, chains, and dungeons are the only means of persuasion employed by keepers who are as barbarous as they are ignorant. (Zilboorg and Henry, 1941, p. 570)

Despite the fact that deplorable conditions such as these were common, little was done to remedy them. But a change was in the offing.

In 1793, a French physician named Phillippe Pinel was appointed director of a large asylum in Paris called the Bicetre. After inspecting the conditions within the hospital, Pinel moved to relieve the plight of its inmates. He approached the French revolutionary government for permission to remove the patients' chains but was received with suspicion and distrust. The government felt that enemies of the people might be hidden among the inmates and feared that they might inadvertently be released with the rest. Nevertheless, Pinel persisted and received his permission; in the same year he assumed the directorship of the Bicetre, the chains were removed from the inmates. This act constituted a major landmark in the institutional treatment of the mentally ill. The results, as history now records, were extremely favorable. The patients were not wild and destructive as many predicted, but instead were thankful and docile. Some who had been interred for decades were even able to leave the hospital a few months later.

Some time afterward, Pinel was asked to administer another large mental hospital, the Salpetriere. Conditions here were as bad as they had been in the Bicetre, with ducking and bloodletting common. Pinel immediately forbade these practices and once again removed the chains from the inmates. He simultaneously persuaded the hospital personnel to treat the patients with dignity. The patients responded remarkably well, once again rewarding his faith in human nature.

The social reforms at the end of the eighteenth century could not have occurred if not for a profound shift in the public's attitude towards abnormal behavior. As long as the demonological model prevailed, the mentally ill could not be treated with kindness or dignity, because to do so would signify a surrender to demonic forces. As the doctrine of demonology faded, the naturalistic model came forth once again after lying fallow for fifteen hundred years.

Even though adoption of the naturalistic model placed the locus of mental illness in body processes, people still did not know much about specific disorders. At the close of the eighteenth century, medical men were still trying to distinguish between different types of disturbances, and treatment techniques remained in their infancy. The period between 1800 and 1900 saw two unique theories of psychopathology develop, each of which was a variation on naturalism. The naturalistic model gave birth, so to speak, to the organic and psychological models that, in turn, ultimately came to represent the period's dominant points of view.

### Organic vs. Psychological Models

The organic model of mental illness firmly places the source of abnormal behavior in either tissue damage or biochemical brain disturbance. Each of these may result from genetic defect, endocrine dysfunction, infection, or injury. Although the organic basis for some disorders, such as alcoholic and senile psychoses, has been discovered, it remains undiscovered for the major mental illnesses such as depression and schizophrenia—if, in fact, organic defects in these syndromes even exist. Many organicists argue that they do but that current instruments lack the sensitivity to detect them. They believe precise chemical tests and accurate surgical techniques will ultimately be developed thereby enabling scientists to discover the physical factors responsible for mental illness.

The psychological model, in contrast, places its emphasis on pathological learning. Abnormal behavior is contingent on deviant patterns of learning that are reflected in a general inability to cope with life's demands. Because of events that typically occur early in life, the mentally ill have not learned how to efficiently gratify their needs or to effectively deal with others. The result is withdrawal into fantasy, development of symptoms, and other abnormal responses.

In surveying the history of abnormal psychology, we find the organic and psychological models competing against one another in both Germany and France, perhaps the two most active centers of psychiatric thought in nineteenth century Europe. In Germany, psychiatrists were trying to solve the puzzle of schizophrenia—a psychotic disorder characterized by illogical speech, bizarre beliefs, and a progressive loss of contact with reality. In France, psychiatrists were devoting equal attention to hysteria—a neurotic disorder featuring puzzling losses of memory and strange paralyses of the limbs. In both countries, the organic and psychological models were pitted against one another, thereby providing us with an excellent opportunity to observe how each developed.

### CONTRIBUTIONS OF GERMAN PSYCHIATRY

German psychiatry for the greater part of the nineteenth century was organic psychiatry. And it was a psychiatry begging for systemization. German clinicians accordingly devoted a great deal of their energy to constructing an organized classification, or *nosology*, of mental illness. The two figures most associated with these pursuits were Wilhelm Griesinger and Emil Kraepelin.

Griesinger is best known for promoting the organic point of view. In *The Pathology and Therapy of Mental Illness* published in 1845, he sets out his major thesis: "Mental illness is a disease of the body, specifically of the brain, and thus is no different from other illnesses." Mental disturbances thus were assimilated into what was becoming the dominant view of illness in the nineteenth century—medical disease theory. According to this theory, every disease is tied to pathology of an organ system and symptoms are merely the surface indications of an underlying disorder. Bodily symptoms arise from diseases of the heart, lungs, kidneys, and other organs; mental symptoms derive from a disease of the brain. In its most basic form, this is the organic model of psychopathology.

To a world still filled with the residual superstitions of demonology, the organic model represented a comforting point of view even though it led to a dead end with regard to treatment. The term "therapy" in the title of Griesinger's text was at best an empty promise; German psychiatry tended to regard most mental disorders as incurable.

Like Griesinger, Kraepelin also subscribed to the assumption of incurable brain pathology. Kraepelin, however, devoted his energies to the creation of a nosology. By carefully sifting through thousands of case studies, he constructed what was to be the most widely accepted classification scheme in psychiatric history. Kraepelin's work is so detailed and complete (the last edition of his work is in two volumes and fills twenty-five hundred pages) that it forms the basis for the classification scheme that is used today by the majority of psychologists and psychiatrists.

One of the disorders described in Kraepelin's nosology was labeled *dementia praecox* (precocious insanity), so named because its onset was thought to occur in adolescence. Dementia praecox (today called schizophrenia) was classified as an incurable disorder that took the course of progressive, irreversible deterioration. In fact, the disorder was largely diagnosed on the basis of its *prognosis*, or outcome. If the patient recovered, it was assumed that the initial diagnosis was in error and that he could not have had dementia praecox to begin with.

This view of dementia praecox was highly compatible with many of the psychiatric discoveries of the day. *Korsakoff's syndrome*, a disorder manifested in bizarre behavior and confused thought, was shown to result from brain damage brought about by alcoholism. *General paresis*, a disorder marked by a variety of psychotic-like symptoms and paralysis, was similarly traced through autopsies to deterioration of brain tissue. Only later was it convincingly demonstrated that general paresis was caused by syphilis. In the meantime, such findings tended to reinforce and perpetuate the organic interpretation of mental illness.

It was not until the early 1900's that the organic view of dementia praecox was challenged by the Swiss psychiatrist Eugen Bleuler, who portrayed the disorder in psychological terms and renamed it *schizophrenia*. Bleuler introduced the term schizophrenia (*schizo* = split, *phrenia* = mind) to describe a severe breakdown in personality functioning brought about by loosened associations. However, it was an unfortunate selection of terms because the word does not mean split personality as commonly believed. It does not refer to anything like a Jekyll-Hyde transformation, but rather to Bleuler's belief that the patient's disturbance stemmed from a separation, or splitting apart, of mental associations. This in turn was held responsible for the patient's distorted beliefs and often incomprehensible speech patterns.

Bleuler went on to construct a relatively sophisticated psychological picture of schizophrenia by carefully describing the associative impairment, interpersonal withdrawal, and bizarre emotional reactions that comprised it. In the process, he showed that many schizophrenics recovered, thereby challenging Kraepelin's contention that all schizophrenics inevitably deteriorated. Bleuler's ability to successfully recast schizophrenia in psychological terms tended to weaken the prestige of the organic model, and helped pave the way for a psychological interpretation of mental disorders.

Although the organic view of mental illness tended to fade at the turn of the century, it did not entirely disappear from view. There are many people who still believe that at least certain mental disturbances, particularly the psychoses, are largely organic in nature. Most of those who maintain that organic factors are involved, however, tend to subscribe to an interaction *hypothesis*. In this view, both organic and environmental factors must be present for a psychiatric disturbance to occur.

The interaction hypothesis is depicted in an article by Paul Meehl, entitled *Schizotaxia, Schizotypy, Schizophrenia* (1962). In this article Meehl argues the presence of an organic deficit in *all* schizophrenics, a deficit he labels *schizotaxia*. Assumed to be genetic in nature, the defect is hypothesized to exert its influence through subtly interfering with the operation of single nerve cells. *Schizotypy* refers to a unique type of personality organization that develops as a result of the organic defect. It is manifested in an individual's inability to experience pleasure and in a tendency to suffer from associative slips. The schizotype, thus, is a person whose emotional reactions tend to be rather flat and lifeless and whose thought processes tend to be somewhat disorganized.

Most schizotypes, nevertheless, do not turn out to be schizophrenics, that is, they do not manifest the clinical symptoms of schizophrenia that invariably attract psychiatric attention. Given a favorable environment and optimal learning conditions, they usually do not actually become psychotic. At best, such individuals may act a bit peculiar or eccentric. It is the small minority of schizotypes who as children were exposed to parental conflict and rejection by others that develop into schizophrenics. In their cases, negative learning experiences have acted on the genetic predisposition to produce the clinical disorder.

But thinking about schizophrenia and mental disturbances was not this sophisticated in the nineteenth century. Although some vague notions of interaction were occasionally voiced, they were before their time and not articulated very well. The leading physicians of the day were biased in an organic direction and it was not until the end of the century that the writing of people such as Bleuler began to be regarded as worthy of attention. At approximately the same time, a series of events were taking place in France that would bolster the psychological point of view. There, the issue of organic vs. psychological etiology revolved about the study of hysteria.

## CONTRIBUTIONS FROM FRENCH PSYCHIATRY

The story of hysteria is unusually complex and has filled volumes by itself. The disorder is characterized by losses of memory and physical symptoms that seem to have no basis in injury or disease. Hysterical patients not only manifest various grades of amnesia but fall victim to paralysis, loss of eyesight or hearing, and skin insensitivities (anesthesias). Throughout history, hysteria has been subject to many different interpretations. In Hippocrates' day, hysteria was thought to result from the uterus leaving its accustomed resting place and settling in the afflicted part of the body (*hysterikos* = Greek for uterus). During the medieval inquisitions, the symptoms of hysteria were taken as indications of demonic possession. It was not until well into the nineteenth century that hysteria was recognized as a psychological disorder, and even then it was surrounded by a great deal of mysticism and controversy.

In 1780, a mystic named Franz Anton Mesmer startled the scientific community by claiming that he could cure numerous disorders by "magnetizing" people. Undoubtedly one of the great charlatans of all times, he convinced a great number of people of the presence of a mysterious, invisible fluid in the universe called animal magnetism. If not evenly distributed within the body, this substance allegedly could cause severe disturbance in a person's behavior. Mesmer treated people suffering from these disturbances (many of whom today we would regard as hysterics) by redistributing their fluids, a feat accomplished by speaking to them in soothing tones and stroking their bodies with metal wands. Surprisingly, some patients did show miraculous recoveries and many more claimed a sense of heightened well-being. Only later did the scientific world conclude that underlying Mesmer's phenomenal cures was a technique called hypnosis.

In the years that followed, hypnotic phenomena drew increasing attention from the medical world. Nevertheless, the precise relationship between hypnotism and hysteria was not uncovered until nearly one hundred years later. In France, a neurologist named Jean-Martin Charcot and a physician named Hippolyte Bernheim independently constructed contrasting theories of the relations between the two phenomena. Once again the organic and psychological models were offered as explanations for an important psychiatric disorder.

Charcot, working in Paris at the Salpetriere, was essentially an organicist. He believed that hysteria was a neurological disease and that its physiological or anatomical origins eventually would be discovered. Charcot had only to explain how hysterical symptoms could be made to appear under hypnosis in patients who had not previously been disturbed. His solution was surprisingly simple. Those who could be hypnotized were also suffering from a subtle organic defect; they too were abnormal! With this conclusive pronouncement, Charcot reconciled all the contradictory evidence and, in so doing, temporarily advanced the cause of the organicists.

Bernheim did not see things in such simple terms. A talented clinician who leaned toward psychological explanations, he noted that both hysterical patients and hypnotizable normals were highly suggestible. Careful study subsequently convinced him that it was, in fact, suggestibility rather than organic deficit that tied hypnosis to hysteria. On the basis of his own observations, Bernheim challenged the validity of Charcot's contentions which were based on unproved organic lesions. In their place he substituted his own psychologically based explanation emphasizing the role of suggestibility.

For the next decade, an ideological battle raged between the two. The bulk of empirical evidence, however, was on Bernheim's side and his point of view eventually prevailed. This marked another important milestone in the growth of the psychological model. Once again, a purely psychological conceptualization was put forth and accepted as an explanation of a major mental disorder.

The work of Charcot and Bernheim did not go unnoticed by the younger physicians of the day. One of these, a young Viennese neurologist, not only studied with Charcot in Paris, but also travelled across France to consult with Bernheim. Impressed with what he saw, Sigmund Freud returned to Austria to apply his newly acquired skills to the treatment of the mentally ill.

In Vienna, Freud joined forces with an older physician named Joseph Breuer, and together they treated hysteria with hypnotism. Although they soon terminated their partnership, it was not before they had collaborated on a book called *Studies in Hysteria* (Breuer and Freud, 1895). The book, a compilation of case studies describing their treatment techniques, today is little more than a psychiatric curiosity. Nevertheless, it contained the faint beginnings of an approach to psychopathology that would revolutionize psychiatric thinking, an approach called *psychoanalysis*.

Freud continued alone and in 1900 published what many consider his most brilliant work, *The Interpretation of Dreams*. This was followed in 1905 by *Three Contributions to the Theory of Sex*, and in 1909 by *Introductory Lectures on Psychoanalysis*. The lectures were delivered at Clark University in Worcester, Massachusetts, during the course of a trip to the United States, and functioned to introduce American psychiatry to Freud's view of abnormal behavior. Along with his writings, the lectures formed the basis for the Freudian, or psychoanalytic, theory of personality —a theory that contained the first comprehensive psychological model of mental disturbance. In this model, learning rather than anatomical lesions or biochemical faults formed the basis for pathological behavior.

At the turn of the twentieth century, the psychological model was rapidly becoming the preferred way of explaining psychopathology. But as we pointed out, the organic model did not simply disappear. It remains with us today, and in its more sophisticated form underlies most studies of the genetic and biochemical correlates of mental illness. In its more reprehensible form, it resides as an unspoken bias among those who still cling to nineteenth century notions of incurability. These latter biases result in custodial institutionalization and "therapeutic" brain surgery, topics that will be considered in more depth in subsequent chapters. We now move on to the twentieth century to survey some of the major contemporary approaches to the study of disordered behavior.

### Intrapsychic and Behavioristic Models

Both the intrapsychic and behavioristic models are outgrowths of the psychological approach to abnormal behavior. Each focuses on learning even though they differ about what is learned and the significant mechanisms involved.

The beginnings of each model can be traced to the first decade of the twentieth century, a period that saw Sigmund Freud and Ivan Pavlov both achieve notable acclaim for their advances in the field of psychology. While Freud was gaining widespread recognition for the theories put forth in *The Interpretation of Dreams*, Pavlov was awarded the Nobel Prize for his work on conditioned reflexes. Both men, in their own way, significantly influenced the manner in which mental illness would be viewed in modern times. Although Pavlov's influence was not felt as directly or as early as Freud's each was the respective architect of the behavioristic and intrapsychic approaches to psychopathology.

The intrapsychic (*intra* = within; *psychic* = mind) model places the locus of psychopathology deep within the personality as a severe character fault or a pervasive conflict. Although variations of the intrapsychic model abound, all subscribe to the basic dictum that abnormal behavior is related to *internal disturbance*, that is, to forces operating within the personality that are in conflict with each other. The behavioristic model derives from experimental work with humans and animals, and represents the application of learning principles to abnormal behavior. Psychopathology within the behavioristic approach is viewed in terms of *maladaptive habits*. Mental disturbance is consequently seen in terms of external behavior rather than internal conflict. Attempts to explain abnormal behavior therefore focus on demonstrable rewards and punishments that control the patient's behavior, and not on unobservable internal states.

CONFLICT AND FIXATION: PSYCHOANALYSIS

Psychoanalysis, the dominant representative of the intrapsychic point of view, is an all-encompassing theory of personality comprised of two interrelated subtheories. One of these concentrates on cognitive functioning, while the other deals with developmental stages of childhood.

Freud's theory of cognitive functioning sees all thought processes as belonging to one of the three mental systems—the id, ego, and superego. The id is the most basic of the three and the one from which the others develop. It is the source of all psychological energy and derives from man's biological instincts. Of these, sexual and aggressive instincts are given the most attention since they are thought to guide much of man's behavior. Briefly stated, the id represents the instinctual, primitive, and therefore irrational side of man. It is the reservoir of man's unconscious urges.

The mental processes of the id, generally speaking, constitute the mental activity of the very young child. Since the infant is helpless and immobile, these processes take the form of wishful fantasies. If the baby cries and the mother cannot come immediately, he conjures up a mental picture of her; if he is hungry and food is not readily available, he creates an image of food. As long as the child is not mobile enough to get what he wants on his own, he must resort to fantasy. But fantasy is a grossly ineffective means of satisfying one's needs. Images of food cannot substitute for milk and bread, at least not for very long. A subsequent set of mental processes develops which is better designed to insure the organism's survival. These are subsumed under the term ego.

The ego is comprised of logical, purposive thought processes that facilitate the individual's transactions with his surroundings. Here we are speaking of planning, problem solving, and other techniques that people must rely upon to help them master their environment. But the ego must also help keep man's impulses in check since overactive expression of sexual and aggressive urges can lead to dire consequences. Society simply does not tolerate rape, assault, and other crimes of impulse. The ego therefore curbs and controls the forces of the id while simultaneously monitoring the individual's interactions with his world.

Finally, we have the superego, a concept used to subsume those mental functions commonly referred to as conscience and guilt. It is a concept symbolizing the child's internalization of adult values, values originally enforced by parental reward and punishment. Our moral attitudes stem from the superego as do our feelings of guilt that follow taboo thoughts and forbidden acts.

As one might imagine, the forces of the superego and the id often are at odds. Unbridled expression of one's urges can conflict with the moral prohibitions that are a part of the superego and lead to uncomfortable repercussions. Freely acting out one's sexual impulses, for example, can result in overwhelming feelings of shame and guilt. Nevertheless, individuals cannot simply suppress all their urges; impulse expression is a natural consequence of life. There obviously has to be some kind of compromise. In the adjusted individual this is precisely what happens; guided by the ego, the various mental agencies reach an accommodation and operate in harmony.

Things, however, do not always go this smoothly, particularly if the ego is not strong. If this is the case, there is apt to be a great deal of internal conflict, the external manifestation of which is pathological behavior. People whose superego is dominant tend to be highly moralistic and self-righteous, and are ill prepared to cope with sexual and aggressive urges. Such persons often develop chronic guilt feelings as well as a variety of other symptoms. Those dominated by their id, on the other hand, may turn out to be narcissistic, self-serving individuals who show little concern for the consequences of their actions. These people will either withdraw from reality and enter private worlds of fantasy, or develop flagrantly antisocial behavior patterns. Only when the ego reigns as the master, or executive, of the personality can the individual lead a relatively smooth, conflict-free existence.

Freud's theory of mental functioning is complemented by his theory of childhood development. This theory traces the young child through a progression of biologically fixed stages, each of which centers about an area of the body that, when stimulated, creates pleasurable sensations. These areas, or *erogenous zones*, tend to dominate at different points in the child's early years, particularly between birth and the age of about five or six. In the *oral stage*, lasting through approximately the second year, the mouth is the prime site of pleasurable stimulation. This is followed in the third and fourth years by the *anal* stage and finally by the *phallic* stage. During this last period, occurring in the fifth and sixth years, genital gratification takes precedence. It is the child's emergent sexuality during this period of development, coupled with his affectionate feeling for his mother, that leads to incestuous complications subsumed under the colorful label Oedipus complex.

The child's progression through the various psychosexual stages entails movement from less to more mature behavior. Sucking in the oral stage is succeeded by drinking from a glass; soiling diapers in the anal stage is replaced by bowel control; and immediate gratification of sexual urges is supplanted by sexual restraints. Successful resolution of the conflicts inherent in each stage (gratification vs. deprivation, freedom vs. restraint) forms the basis for psychological maturity.

Each stage, unfortunately, holds within it the potential for serious psychic pitfalls and future psychological difficulty. If the child is overly frustrated (socialized harshly or prematurely) *or* overindulged (allowed extensive and prolonged gratification), he may become psychologically stuck at a particular point in the sequence. In the former case, the child seeks to acquire what he never had; in the second case, he tries desperately not to lose it. Persistence of these tendencies into adulthood is referred to as *fixation*. Characterized as a psychological predisposition marked by immature attitudes and feelings of frustration, fixation often culminates in behavior that is developmentally inappropriate. The unfinished business of childhood has persisted into the present so that immature responses are now the rule rather than the exception.

The concept of fixation is used to explain a wide variety of abnormal behavior that otherwise might remain incomprehensible. The problem of a patient who suffers from impotency, for example, would be explained in terms of fixation at the phallic stage. Sexual feelings toward women in the patient's current life cannot be detached from erotic feelings directed earlier toward the mother, feelings that initially emerged in the phallic stage of development. The result is excessive guilt that the patient cannot explain but that nevertheless interferes with his sexual functioning.

Freud's theory of developmental stages, combined with his theory of conflicting mental processes, comprises the psychoanalytic version of the intrapsychic model. In this model, the source of psychiatric disturbance is placed within the individual—in an inner psychic struggle between infantile urges and forces that oppose their expression. Symptoms merely reflect this struggle; they are seen as surface indications of a deeper disturbance in the same way that physical symptoms are viewed as indices of an underlying disorder in the field of medicine. Because of this parallel, the psychoanalytic approach sometimes is referred to as the medical model of psychopathology.

Freud's intrapsychic model has undergone some revisions, much of which can be traced to the work of his disciples. The *Neo-Freudians*, represented by Alfred Adler, Harry Stack Sullivan, Eric Fromm and others, emphasized interpersonal and cultural factors, and came to typify the social branch of psychoanalytic thought. The *Ego analysts*, represented by Heinz Hartmann and Erik Erikson, developed formulations of personality centering about the ego, guided by the conviction that Freud had overemphasized the importance of unconscious motives and instinctual drives. Despite all this, Freud's basic theory continued to hold sway as the dominant representative of the intrapsychic school of thought. Toward the middle of the twentieth century, however, another model was claiming widespread professional interest.

STIMULUS AND RESPONSE:
LEARNING AND PSYCHOPATHOLOGY

The behavioristic model, as we indicated earlier, had its beginnings in the work of Ivan Pavlov. Pavlov's interest in abnormal behavior led him to conduct some of the earliest studies in experimental psychopathology. Specifically, he demonstrated that it was possible to induce behavioral disorganization in dogs by subjecting them to severe, inescapable conflict. But it was not this particular research that led to Pavlov's impact in the area of psychopathology. Instead it was his pioneering work on conditioned responses. Here Pavlov demonstrated that it was possible to teach an animal to salivate simply on the presentation of a bell or a light (conditioned stimuli). This caught the attention of John Watson, an American psychologist, who startled the scientific community by experimentally creating a neurosis in the laboratory.

Watson, in the celebrated case of "Little Albert," sought to demonstrate that an irrational fear, or *phobia,* could be learned in much the same way that other behavior is learned. To accomplish this, he exposed a small child, Albert, to a white laboratory rat while simultaneously striking a metal bar with a hammer to produce a startling noise. Albert thus was subjected to repeated pairings of the rat with the noxious sound. Although Albert originally was unafraid of the rat, he soon came to fear the animal, even when it no longer was paired with the noise. The child's fearful reaction to the noise (the unconditioned response) was thereby conditioned to the previously neutral rat (the conditioned stimulus). Little Albert, through an experimental manipulation, had acquired a phobia. Watson subsequently demonstrated that the conditioned fear generalized since Albert later developed a fear of other furry stimuli such as rabbits and fur coats.

Some years following Watson's demonstration, John Dollard and Neal Miller collaborated in an effort to integrate the contributions of psychoanalysis with the principles of learning theory. In 1950, they published *Personality and Psychotherapy,* in which the different syndromes of psychopathology were analyzed via learning concepts such as reinforcement, extinction, and stimulus generalization. Although Dollard and Miller accepted some of the basic premises of psychoanalytic thought, such as the childhood origin of neurosis, they demonstrated how much of what we call psychopathology could be explained by a limited number of rigorously defined learning principles.

In recent years, the application of learning theory to abnormal psychology has been reflected most clearly in the work of Joseph Wolpe, a psychiatrist who has applied behavioristic techniques to the treatment of phobias. Wolpe sees the learning process underlying the development of phobias as essentially the same as that underlying the conditioning of animals. Just as Pavlov's dogs irrationally salivate at the sound of a bell, so some human beings become irrationally anxious in the presence of certain stimuli. A phobia, in Wolpe's eyes, simply is the end result of a series of unfortunate associations between *anxiety responses* (rapid breathing, tense musculature, cold sweats) and harmless *anxiety stimuli* (the phobic objects). Thus, the individual who has an insect phobia automatically experiences anxiety whenever he encounters anything from a cricket to a cockroach. Since his *response* is automatically bonded to the phobic *stimuli,* anxiety is evoked whenever he thinks about or sees insects.

Within the behavioristic model, little effort is spent trying to formulate pathological behavior in terms of early childhood conflicts. Explanations are couched in terms of conditioning rather than in terms of fixation or unconscious motives. The behaviorist focuses on the symptom, for in this approach, the symptom is the illness. Hans Eysenck, a leading behaviorist, summarizes this point of view: "Learning theory . . . regards neurotic symptoms as simple learned habits; there is no neurosis underlying the symptom but merely the symptom itself. *Get rid of the symptom and you have eliminated the neurosis*" (1960, p. 9).

Many behaviorally oriented clinicians have fashioned their work after B.F. Skinner's theory of operant conditioning. According to Skinner, learning usually takes place when a behaviorial response is followed by a reward, or *reinforcement*. To understand the learning process, one needs only to study the relationship between a person's actions and the reinforcement he subsequently receives.

Abnormal behavior, being learned, is analyzed in essentially the same way. Psychopathology is thought to be maintained because of certain environmental stimuli that act as reinforcers. In the case of a child who has a school phobia, for example, the clinician searches for whatever sustains the phobic behavior. In some cases, it simply turns out to be an over-concerned parent who is providing the child with an inordinate amount of attention because of his "illness." Attention thus is viewed as the reinforcer that sustains the psychopathology, i.e., the child's aversion to school.

As in the case of the classical conditioning approach, major emphasis in the operant school also is placed on the "how" rather than the "why" of pathological behavior. Symptoms again are focused upon with no attempt to search for underlying conflicts. It is this distinction which sets the intrapsychic and behavioristic models so sharply apart. From the intrapsychic point of view, symptoms are only a sign of a more pervasive, malignant disorder; it is imperative therefore to study the personality in depth in order to get at the root of the difficulty. From the behaviorist's vantage point, it is necessary only to study observable surface behaviors; little else is needed to understand and treat psychological disturbances. The controversy today is still a heated one.

Which of these contemporary models is correct? Does one provide a better way of looking at abnormal behavior than the other? These are not easy questions to answer. Human beings are so complex that different models may prove equally effective depending upon the specific disorder under consideration. Behavioristic treatment may be the treatment of choice for phobic disorders but quite inappropriate for handling severe depression. It thus is conceivable that each approach will ultimately carve out its own special area of expertise.

It is also entirely possible that one of these models will eventually predominate or that both will be phased out by a more sophisticated approach. Perhaps this is inevitable in any field where new data and new insights must continually be assimilated. How long will it take? Considering that it took fifteen hundred years for a theory as fantastic as demonology to fade out of the picture, we would be wise not to hold our breaths.

We conclude by pointing out that our goal in this chapter has been to chart the transformations that have taken place in man's conception of abnormal behavior over the centuries. This perspective is schematically portrayed in Figure 4. It has been our contention that current views of abnormal behavior have resulted not from sudden insights, but from a slow evolutionary process in which different models of psychopathology competed as alternative explanations for puzzling human phenomena. We further suggested that the treatment of pathological behavior derives directly from certain assumptions embedded in each model, a hypothesis to be explored more fully in a later chapter. We now turn our attention, however, to the disorders that comprise the syndromes of abnormal behavior.

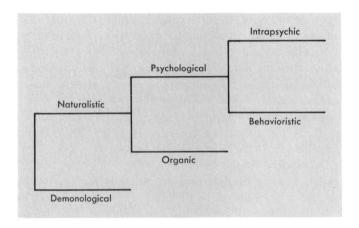

FIGURE 4.  Models of abnormal behavior.

# Syndromes of Abnormal Behavior

## chapter two

The realm of psychopathology is extremely broad and encompasses a variety of disorders. Some are relatively rare whereas others are so common they are a subject of national concern. Although an occasional disorder is identified by a single predominant symptom, most are represented in a number of symptoms. Among the symptoms included in a diagnosis of psychotic depression, for example, are physical weariness, feelings of guilt, restlessness, and suicidal impulses. Similar groupings could be specified for most other mental disturbances, with each group of symptoms referred to as a *syndrome*.

The various pathological syndromes fall into one of several major categories. One is *mental retardation*. The primary symptom in this category is subnormal intellect, although physical defects such as facial deformity and poor motor coordination also are common. *Organic disorders* form a second major group. The main criterion for inclusion in this category is damage to brain tissue or impairment of the brain's biochemistry. Finally there are *functional disorders*. In these, psychological factors play a primary role. Comprised of neurosis, sociopathy, and psychosis, this category constitutes the largest class of mental disorders.

In the following pages, functional disturbances are focused upon and described in detail. We examine each of these syndromes not only from the clinician's perspective but from the patient's vantage point as well. Wherever possible, first person accounts are introduced to illustrate the ways in which these disorders are subjectively experienced by the mentally ill.

## Neurotic Disorders

The symptoms that constitute neurotic disorders are quite varied and range from vague feelings of apprehension to inexplicable losses of memory. Symptoms such as these are sometimes not very different from the occasional anxiety and minor lapses of memory that plague normals. But in the case of a neurotic patient, they have become overly disruptive and sometimes disabling. Furthermore, they usually emerge out of a background of persistent anxiety, insecurity, and unsatisfactory interpersonal relationships.

Despite the severity of his symptoms and the disruptive effects of anxiety, a neurotic is able to maintain a reasonable degree of contact with the environment. There is little distortion of reality, and hospitalization is ordinarily uncalled for. Most neurotics continue to meet prescribed cultural expectations and fulfill most of their responsibilities—they maintain their family relationships, keep their jobs, or stay in school. Nevertheless symptoms and anxiety prevent them from functioning as smoothly as they otherwise might.

The symptoms that comprise neurotic disturbances are grouped within several different categories. *Anxiety neuroses* are those in which specific fears and vague feelings of apprehension are the most common complaints. In *obsessive–compulsive neuroses* the patient not only is bothered by incessant thoughts but compelled to behave in strange, ritualistic ways. Finally, in *hysterical neuroses*, physical symptoms and memory losses play a prominent role.

### ANXIETY NEUROSES

In this category, anxiety occurs either as a response to specific stimuli or as a general state of apprehension. We refer to the first condition as a *phobia*, and to the second as an *anxiety reaction*.

In phobic disturbances the patient is terribly frightened of certain objects or situations but cannot comprehend the reason for his fear. Some phobic patients are terrified of cats or dogs, others are fearful of insects; many patients develop extreme anxiety in tall buildings and others get panicky in enclosed spaces. Whatever the circumstances, neurotics in this category are able to control their irrational fears only by avoiding phobic situations, something they often find difficult to acomplish.

Phobias can develop in response to a wide range of stimuli that in themselves are not usually frightening. Specific phobias derive their names from the source of anxiety—for example, *zoophobia* (fear of animals), *acrophobia* (fear of heights), *claustrophobia* (fear of closed spaces), *agoraphobia* (fear of open spaces), and so on.

One of the most common phobias is depicted in *The Locomotive God* (1927), an autobiographical account of agoraphobia written by a University of Wisconsin English professor named William Leonard. The author describes an intense fear of open spaces, a fear that lasted for many years and prevented him from going very far from his home. His "distance phobia," as he labeled it, eventually forced him to move into an apartment across the street from the university just so he could be closer to the classes he taught. In one brief passage, Leonard vividly describes the emotional experience associated with his phobia:

> For the emotion in the distance-phobia, as for the emotion in all others, there have been clearly defined degrees of intensity. Let me assume that I am walking down the University Drive by the Lake. I am a normal man for the first quarter of a mile; for the next hundred yards I am in a mild state of dread, controllable and controlled; for the next twenty yards in an acute state of dread, yet controlled; for the next ten, in an anguish of terror that hasn't reached the crisis of explosion; and in a half-dozen steps more I am in as fierce a panic of isolation of help and home and of immediate death as a man overboard in mid-Atlantic or on a window ledge far up in a skyscraper with flames lapping his shoulders. (p. 321–22)

Leonard attributed his phobia to an incident in his childhood in which he wandered away from home and was frightened by the noise of a passing locomotive. This knowledge apparently was of little value to him; his phobia lasted most of his adult life.

Whether a patient fears open spaces, closed spaces, spiders, or snakes, the anxiety in a phobia can at least be tied to something in the environment. The same cannot be said for an anxiety reaction; here the patient also experiences severe anxiety, but the source remains unknown. No matter how hard the patient tries, he cannot uncover the reason for his discomfort.

An anxiety reaction can adopt the form of chronic nervousness or intermittent anxiety attacks. Whatever form it takes, it represents an extreme exaggeration of normal anxiety. The vague apprehensive feelings we all experience at one time or another are magnified tenfold in anxiety reactions. This is seen in the following case study:

The twenty-six-year-old wife of a successful lawyer came to a psychiatric clinic with the complaint that she had "the jitters". . . . She suffered from constant headache, fatigue, and nervousness, from episodes of abdominal cramps, and diarrhea. Twice in the past year there had been "attacks," in which she had become dizzy and had broken out into a cold sweat. Her hands and feet became clammy, her heart pounded, her head seemed tight, she had a lump in her throat and could not get her breath. One of these attacks occurred in the middle of the night when her husband was out of town. She awoke crying and shaking violently, and remembered thinking in terror, "I'm sick here alone and my husband is away and nobody knows who I am." As she related her symptoms at the clinic, the patient kept reiterating that her behavior was foolish. "I make such a fuss, but I can't help it," she said. (Cameron and Margaret, 1951, p. 307)

It is the inability to discriminate what is making one anxious that is the earmark of an anxiety reaction. The result is a perplexed, disturbed person who experiences chronic anxiety but cannot meaningfully relate it to anything. In sum, anxiety reactions and phobias differ in the degree to which personal discomfort can be tied to specific stimuli. In both syndromes, anxiety remains the major indication of personal distress.

### OBSESSIVE—COMPULSIVE NEUROSES

Obsessions and compulsions are actually two distinct forms of abnormal behavior. Obsessions are bothersome *ideas* that regularly interrupt one's train of thought; compulsions, in contrast, are ritualistic *actions* that neurotic individuals say they must perform. Although both types of behavior are often seen separately, they frequently appear together.

Obsessions in their milder forms are everyday occurrences. The vacationing housewife's recurrent thought of a water faucet left running at home and the moviegoer's nagging fear that his car's headlights are on, are two common examples. To these can be added more disturbing obsessions dealing with mutilation and death that are not as uncommon as one might think. The following excerpts were solicited from normal college students who were asked to relate any "fixed ideas" they could remember. One recalled:

When I was about eight years of age . . . I thought I was going to cut my throat from ear to ear with a certain large butcher knife in my grandmother's kitchen. I couldn't throw off the idea. . . . I was afraid to go near the knife.

Another responded:

When I am at a railway station watching a train come in I have a desire to jump in front of it and I never have been able to get rid of this feeling. The same thing happened when I saw Niagara Falls this summer. I felt as though something were urging me to jump into them. (Berry, 1916, pp. 19–22)

When obsessive thoughts become pervasive and continually interrupt one's ongoing activity, we enter the realm of neurosis. Here obsessive thoughts are frequently accompanied by overwhelming anxiety. This combination of intrusive thoughts and persistent anxiety obviously imposes a heavy burden.

Some neurotics, in order to deal with severe anxiety of this sort, try to substitute harmless words or jingles in the place of threatening, obsessive thoughts. But this too can have negative consequences:

> At night I was driven to distraction by thoughts of self-destruction—not by the wish to do so but an accurate representation of suicide in various unpleasant ways—and I took elaborate precautions to guard against this. Silly jingles and rhyming phrases said themselves over and over again in my head. Every now and then, of course, all this boiled up to an unbearable intensity. (*Lancet*, editors of, 1951, pp. 84–85)

*Obsessions*, then, are recurrent thoughts that are always extremely bothersome and sometimes very terrifying. Nevertheless, they are typically not acted upon and usually remain ideas and urges. When they are translated into action, we then speak of compulsions.

A *compulsion* is a rigid, sometimes ritualistic, act characterized by an intense, driven quality. Compulsions, like obsessions, are very common phenomena and not always pathological. The housewife who must clean the rooms in her home in a fixed order, the child who must recite a secret chant before he takes a bath, and the adult who finds it necessary to step on every crack in the sidewalk—all display compulsive behavior patterns.

Although the line between normal and abnormal compulsions is blurred, psychopathology is suspect when an individual's actions begin to interfere with his ability to successfully carry out everyday functions. This is demonstrated in the following case:

> A patient interviewed in the outpatient clinic of a large psychiatric hospital told of an irresistible urge to collect empty cereal boxes. A bachelor who lived alone in a small room, he stored the boxes under his bed, in corners, and in his closet. Since he lived alone, he was able to do this without drawing much attention to himself. Eventually, however, thousands of these containers were amassed, and he literally began to crowd himself out of his living quarters. The patient's living habits were forced to change as he found that he could no longer eat or dress in his room. In time this became more and more upsetting and he consequently sought psychiatric help.

This is an example of how a patient's compulsion can grow out of proportion and begin to seriously threaten his daily routine. It is at this point that many individuals begin to acknowledge that their idiosyncracies are more than just minor quirks and decide to seek professional help.

Compulsive behavior that has grown out of control is rigid, compelling, and unavoidable. Compulsive neurotics report that they are driven to behave the way they do, that if they do not comply they become extremely anxious. This is seen in the case of a forty-year-old woman whose fear of germs and contamination by others resulted in a severe washing compulsion:

> In order to find peace, I wash everything in soapy water and, depend-
> ing on the circumstances, I also wash the dress which I wore. . . . If I
> go shopping and someone is in the store, I cannot go in, because I might
> either be pushed by the people there, or receive the money that had
> belonged to them. Thus I am anxious the whole day and this anxiety
> drives me hither and yon. Now I have to wipe away or wash something
> here, then over there . . . I do not find peace anywhere. (Straus, 1938)

This case is instructive in that it highlights one of the most formidable features of neurosis. A neurotic symptom, even though it is designed to alleviate anxiety, creates its own anxiety. The patient's attempts to reduce whatever anxiety the symptom itself produces only leads him back to his original means of anxiety reduction—the neurotic symptom.

An analogous process is seen in heavy cigarette smokers. Many smokers regularly light up whenever they get a little nervous or ill at ease, claiming that a smoke helps calm them; smoking in such instances thus represents one of the dominant techniques by which smokers reduce their anxiety. However, the link between smoking and lung cancer, emphysema, and heart disease is well publicized, and even if an habitual smoker has not read the Surgeon General's report, he certainly has been exposed to the increasing number of antismoking commercials on radio and TV. The act of smoking therefore cannot help but create its own anxiety. And how does an habitual smoker typically reduce this anxiety? By lighting up! The circle is closed and the sequence is ready to be repeated. Applying this formulation to the understanding of compulsive behavior helps us understand why such behavior tends to be self-perpetuating, and why neurotic patients find it so difficult to break out of their maladaptive behavior patterns.

Despite the difficulties caused by obsessions and compulsions, many such patients are able to maintain some semblance of normal functioning. The same cannot be said for patients in the next category of neurosis; the symptoms of hysteria are usually so disruptive they often become incapacitating.

### HYSTERICAL NEUROSES

Hysterical neuroses occupy a prominent position in the history of abnormal psychology because of their dramatic symptomatology. Hysterical blindness, deafness, paralysis, amnesia, and skin anesthesias are just a few of the symptoms that comprise these syndromes. What makes these symptoms so striking is the fact that they have no basis in physical injury or nerve damage. Nevertheless, symptoms such as these are not faked. Hysterically blind individuals, for example, are as unable to see as those who are truly blind. But in. hysterical neurosis, the symptom is rooted in psychological rather than organic disturbance.

Hysteria, it will be recalled, was the disorder on which Freud based his theory of psychoanalysis. According to Freud, the hysterical symptom was a symbolic representation of an underlying, unresolved conflict, one usually having to do with the occurrence of a sexual threat in childhood. A paralyzed hand, for example, might symbolically represent early conflicts over masturbation; hysterical blindness might result from closing one's eyes to an early traumatic sexual episode, perhaps one in which the child accidentally witnessed his parents having intercourse. Whatever the precise circumstances, the symptom, according to psychoanalysis, is derived from an early conflict of sexual origins.

One need not subscribe to psychoanalysis, however, to make sense of hysterical phenomena. Many of the symptoms that are considered hysterical can be viewed as indirect forms of communication that transmit messages about current conflicts, conflicts not necessarily dealing with sexuality. Something of this nature is portrayed in the following case study:

> A young woman suffering from acute difficulty in swallowing was brought to a rural community mental health center by her husband. In the course of brief psychotherapy it was learned that the patient and her husband, a local farmer, had a fairly comfortable, satisfactory relationship. The husband was somewhat of a dependent person and his wife derived a great deal of enjoyment ministering to his needs.
>
> All this drastically changed one day when the husband's mother suddenly arrived for an indefinite stay. The patient's position vis-à-vis the husband was quickly pre-empted by her domineering mother-in-law, who began taking over the household. The wife's one mild complaint to her husband was met with "mother only wants the best for us"; she therefore decided not to press the matter any further. Her symptom developed a few weeks later.
>
> The meaning of the patient's disorder became obvious during therapy as she explored her relationship with the mother-in-law. In these sessions she was able to express her resentment (which at first she denied) and admitted that she was tired of "swallowing what my mother-in-law was handing out."

The symptom was alleviated slightly during treatment and disappeared entirely when the patient's mother-in-law decided to return to her own home. It is not difficult to see that the patient's symptom functioned to symbolically communicate what she could not declare openly.

In other cases involving hysterical symptoms, the relationship between psychological conflicts and their physical representations is not as clear. Perhaps this is because we actually know very little regarding the mechanism by which verbal expressions of emotion and thought are physically expressed. Our language is replete with such phrases as "choked up with emotion," "pain in the neck," "can't stand the sight of him," and so on, and people do develop difficulty swallowing, turning their heads, or seeing clearly. But the "language of the body" is still largely a mystery. What we do know, however, is that many symptoms often help a patient avoid a threatening situation or help to curtail the potential development of anxiety.

Another kind of neurotic disturbance in this category is hysterical amnesia. In this disorder, varying degrees of memory loss disrupt the patient's ongoing behavior and in some instances cause serious discontinuities in his identity. Hysterical amnesia in its least noticeable form results in the blotting out of some episode whose recall would cause anxiety. The soldier who cannot remember the day he went out on a dangerous patrol, and the jilted suitor who cannot recall the circumstances under which he and his fiance broke their engagement, are two examples of mild functional amnesia. In both instances, a sudden inability to recall certain facts or a traumatic episode keeps the individual from confronting truths that might be embarrassing or otherwise anxiety-provoking.

In some cases, amnesia becomes more widespread and results in radically different behavior that the patient later cannot recall. An example of this is seen in a *fugue state*. In this disorder, the patient flees his accustomed surroundings, lives a different existence for days, weeks, or months, and then suddenly comes to, not knowing where he is or how he got there. In some cases his memory spontaneously returns; in other cases his plight comes to the attention of local authorities who bring him home. It is impossible to gauge how many missing persons, thought to be runaways, are actually victims of fugue states. The following episode portrays the puzzlement that is associated with this syndrome:

> With an assurance to my wife that I would be back in a minute or two, I went out and failed to return. . . . I had a feeling of puzzlement upon my mind, not unlike that which one may experience on waking from a deep sleep in a strange place. Where was I? Who was I? Something was wrong, but what was it? . . . I had already realized that something extraordinary had happened to me, but I still felt as though I might wake up at any minute and find the whole thing a dream. It was some minutes before I realized fully that I had absolutely no recollection of any course of events which could have brought me to the existing position. The immediate past seemed to be "a perfect and absolute blank" . . . (Anon., 1932*b*, pp. 16–18).

Even though a patient in a fugue state is amnesiac for extended periods of time, he can almost always resume normal functioning once his memory is regained. Something quite different occurs in the case of *multiple personality*. Here the individual fluctuates between two or more different existences, in effect leading several different lives. Although these disorders are very rare, they command a great deal of attention because of their dramatic qualities.

Perhaps the best known case of multiple personality has been popularized by two psychiatrists named Thigpen and Cleckley. In *The Three Faces of Eve* (1957), they draw an intriguing picture of a young married woman who manifested three separate personalities. The first, Eve White, was a prim, conservative, and highly moralistic woman who could best be described as a paragon of virtue. Her nemesis, Eve Black, was relatively unprincipled and impulsive, a seductive character who gravitated toward fun and adventure. These were balanced by Jane, the most responsible and mature of the three. In contrast to the others, Jane's existence was relatively trouble-free and filled with potential for gratifying relationships. Throughout this fascinating case study the three different personalities warred against one another, each trying desperately to exert its will. The conflict that prompted the development of the disorder eventually was resolved through psychiatric help with Jane adopting the ascendant role.

It does not require too great a stretch of the imagination to see that Eve Black, Eve White, and Jane are anthropomorphic versions of the id, superego, and ego. The impulsivity of Eve Black, the moralistic demeanor of Eve White, and the maturity of Jane represent little more than Freud's view of intrapsychic functioning depicted in social terms. The unique story of this woman's struggle to deal with her different personalities is not very different from the more general story of intrapsychic conflict as depicted in psychoanalytic theory. Just as the three faces of Eve battled with each other for control of the total organism, so do the internal forces that we give the labels id, ego, and superego.

In surveying the different neurotic syndromes, we have covered a wide variety of behaviors, many of which seem to have little relation to one another. Nevertheless careful examination reveals that the various syndromes, ranging from phobias to hysterical amnesias, appear to represent ways in which a patient experiences and deals with anxiety. Anxiety thus seems to play a central role in the development and continuation of neurotic behavior.

The precise way in which anxiety is construed, that is, its origins and functions, as well as the interpretation of symptomatic behavior, is a function of the model to which one subscribes. According to intrapsychic, psychoanalytic doctrine, a neurotic symptom represents an indirect way of discharging unconscious tensions. The human organism, it will be recalled, is viewed as an entity that constantly generates and discharges sexual and aggressive energy. If this energy is not effectively discharged through overt behavior, it can dam up and cause unending, unberable tension. Neurotic individuals, because of negative experiences in childhood, have not learned how to properly discharge tensions without incurring strong feelings of guilt. The symptom is a symbolic means of discharging tensions associated with impulses that cannot be directly expressed or openly confronted.

Thus, in the case of an obsessive–compulsive patient, for example, tension is periodically discharged through a series of repetitive acts such as collecting objects or compulsive hand washing. Such activities symbolically represent unresolved conflicts regarding the expression of impulses that arose during the anal stage, and that revolved about orderliness and cleanliness. The persistence of such conflicts into the present (explained through the concept of fixation) cause anxiety and lead to the development of the symptom. As long as the patient carries out his ritualistic exercises, he can control the buildup of anxiety. The price that he pays, however, is the neurotic symptom.

In the behavioristic model, neurotic symptoms are not viewed as symbolic occurrences but as learned behavior that has grown out of a concrete set of circumstances. Although variations exist, depending on the version of the behavioristic model one adopts (classical vs. operant) and the syndrome one focuses upon, most neurotic symptoms are seen in terms of avoidance behavior. Phobic behavior thus is regarded as an attempt to avoid certain simuli because of an earlier episode in which such stimuli were associated with anxiety. Obsessive–compulsive symptoms are apt to be explained as strongly ingrained distraction techniques. The child who is continually berated or physically punished at the dinner table may learn to excuse himself to go to the bathroom and wash as a means of minimizing anxiety. Later in life, hand washing may be automatically invoked whenever the patient begins to feel anxious. Psychopathology thus results from a conditioning sequence in which certain behavior effectively reduced anxiety. Its persistence into the present is simply a matter of overlearning and has nothing at all to do with an underlying conflict or its symbolic representation.

## Sociopathic Disorders

The sociopathic syndromes, consisting of chronic delinquency, drug dependence, and sexual deviance, have been the subject of clinical speculation for many years. Up until the late 1800's, anyone who fell into these categories was designated as a criminal or an incorrigible. Although some were occasionally treated humanely, most were punished severely. But regardless of what was done to them, or for them, they did not change.

Clinicians, unable to explain such refractory behavior, attributed it to a subtle form of brain damage.

With the growth of the psychological model, organic interpretations of asocial behavior became less and less popular. Deviant conduct began to be regarded not as an outgrowth of brain damage but as the result of learning. As psychologists and psychiatrists studied sociopathic disorders more intensively, they concluded that the specific nature of the sociopath's learning deficit revolved about a lack of moral development. A sociopathic individual, it seemed, had not assimilated the type of learning that was necessary for the development of what we call conscience. Individuals of this sort not only demonstrated a peculiar insensitivity to society's rules, but appeared to show little guilt or remorse after committing misdeeds.

The behavior of a sociopathic patient tends to be quite unpredictable and often incomprehensible. He may lie when it is easier to tell the truth and steal when there is no apparent profit motive. Sometimes his deviant acts are carried out in secret, as in certain types of sexual deviance; other times he will ostentatiously flaunt his arrogance and rebelliousness. No matter what form his behavior takes, it is marked by one unmistakable stamp—the blatant disregard for social convention. It is this one characteristic that places chronic delinquency, drug abuse, and sexual deviance, the three major groups of sociopathy, under the same diagnostic roof.

## CHRONIC DELINQUENCY

The term "delinquency" denotes a variety of legal and ethical violations ranging from car theft and check forging to cheating at cards. Although delinquency does not always involve violation of the law, those sociopathic delinquents who are lawbreakers tend to manifest chronic recidivism patterns; that is, they are continually in and out of jail. A large number, however, are skillful enough to avoid extended stays in prison. Poised on the fringes of society, they sustain themselves by exploiting the vulnerability and feelings of others.

In this group are the con man, dope pusher, and pimp. The common denominator underlying their behavior seems to be a detached, unfeeling attitude toward other human beings. The businesslike stance of the procurer towards his prostitutes, the cool detachment of the pusher for the junkies who rely upon him, and the callous disregard of the con man for those whose life savings he appropriates, all mirror this attitude. The minimal degree of sympathy, compassion, and human warmth that we expect to find in most human beings seems to be absent in sociopathic delinquents.

Asocial attitudes such as those described, however, are not restricted to pimps, pushers, and con men. They are also present among respectable sociopaths—unethical attorneys, doctors, and businessmen who risk the well-being of their clients and associates to satisfy their own selfish needs. Like those sociopaths who operate on the shadier side of the tracks, they also are deficient when it comes to showing true compassion or forming meaningful relationships. In the following case study, we see repeated evidence of this sort of deficiency.

> This young man in his early twenties comes from a respected and prominent family in a small Southern town. . . . During his school years he became a serious problem because of continual truancy, disorderly activity in the classroom, and what appeared to be rebellious conduct in general. . . . Before he was twelve years old it had become a common practice for him to steal things from his home and sell them in the town. Occasionally he took a watch or a piece of his mother's jewelry, and for these relatively valuable objects he was content to accept a dollar or even fifty cents. Sometimes he exercised true ingenuity in concealing his guilt, but again he did not trouble to hide acts that would obviously lead to detection. . . . While in the teens he began to steal automobiles, and his father, seeking to satisfy what one might presume to be the impulse behind this conduct, bought him an automobile of his own. This did not deter him. On one occasion, he actually stopped while riding in his personal car, parked it, and drove off in another. He soon abandoned the stolen car without having achieved any financial or other discernible gain from it. . . .
>
> His relations with women have been indiscriminate and apparently without any serious attachment on his part. His outer charm and what resembles a deep earnestness have enabled him to seduce a number of women regarded as respectable, including the wife of a friend who at the time was fighting overseas. He has consorted freely with cheap prostitutes, and a few years ago married one whom he had previously shared in a single night with drinking acquaintances. He left her as abruptly and with as little sense of obligation as he did the women of good reputation whom he seduced.
>
> People who talked with him after disasters overtook him, or when he was seeking leniency from the courts, were invariably impressed with him. Several of these advisers, including judges, physicians, and clergymen, not only felt that he was a man of remarkable ability who had at last found himself and who would now conduct himself admirably, but even confessed that he was able to give them new points of view and make them hope to improve their own lives. After every incident of this sort he immediately returned to the familiar pattern. (Cleckley, 1948, pp. 259–60)

In cases similar to this, efforts at rehabilitation typically prove futile. Sociopaths usually are not distressed over their misbehavior; the requisite motivation for treatment, therefore, is lacking. If therapeutic change does occur, it tends to be superficial and shortlived.

Since sociopaths frequently break the law and often have to face criminal prosecution, what distinguishes sociopathic from nonsociopathic criminals? This obviously is a complex question involving definitions of criminality and mental illness, as well as personal values. Perhaps part of the answer lies in the motives we attribute to persons who commit criminal acts and the effect that punishment has on them.

If a violation of the law appears to be motivated by profit, anger, or revenge, we tend to see it as ordinary criminal behavior. If the behavior is repetitive in nature and seems to be motivated by a guilt-ridden need to be caught and punished, we are apt to label it neurotic. The latter often is the case in compulsive shoplifting, or kleptomania (*klepto*=to steal; *mania*=madness). If, however, a criminal act is accompanied by senseless violence or appears to have been carried out just for kicks, we tend to consider it sociopathic.

The term "sociopathy" is reserved for behavior that is neither neurotic nor psychotic but that nevertheless is characterized by senselessness and impulsivity. Thus, if a hold-up man mercilessly beats his victim *after* he has taken his money, or a well-to-do executive embezzles funds that he does not need, the acts are likely to be termed sociopathic. And if the person in question is apprehended but continues along the same path after he is punished, seemingly unaffected by his lesson, our initial diagnosis of sociopathy is apt to be confirmed.

Although much of the delinquent sociopath's behavior is purposeless and self-defeating, it would be unwise to label him stupid or inept; such individuals, as we saw in the preceding case study, may be very facile in their social interactions. They also score at average or above-average levels on standard intelligence tests. A sociopath in many instances knows the correct way to behave. What we are witnessing, then, is an inability or an unwillingness to conform to minimal societal standards. It is this recalcitrant type of behavior that ultimately leads to mental hospitalization or imprisonment.

DRUG ABUSE

Drugs are one of the most widely discussed and controversial topics of our time—and also one of the most confusing. Terms such as addiction, abuse, and dependence constantly appear in the newspaper and on TV, and are often so tied up in highly charged emotional issues that their meanings are distorted. In order to make sense of the welter of confusion that surrounds the subject of drug abuse, we will follow the recommendation of the World Health Organization and center our discussion on the concepts of psychological and physical dependence.

Psychological dependence, or *habituation*, is implicated in practically every case of sustained drug use. Dependence of this sort has no basis in the body's physiochemistry but nevertheless can be quite compelling. It leads to a strong psychological craving for the drug substance as well as to feelings of jitteriness and emptiness whenever the drug is withheld. Psychological dependence lies behind the nicotine fits of the heavy cigarette smoker, the depression of the speed (methadrine) freak, and the nervousness of the heavy drinker.

Physical dependence, or *addiction*, is defined by two related but somewhat independent phenomena: tolerance and the presence of an abstinence syndrome. *Tolerance* refers to a drug's ability, upon continuous use, to alter the body's biochemistry such that progressively larger dosages are required to create the same effect produced earlier by smaller doses. The alcoholic thus requires a pint of liquor or more a day to produce the same effect that he obtained earlier with a shot or two; the narcotic addict needs five bags of heroin a day to experience the high that he once achieved with one bag. A drug's ability to produce tolerance does not necessarily mean that it causes physical dependence. Practically every drug produces tolerance if it is used daily. For there to be addiction, there also must be an abstinence syndrome.

An *abstinence syndrome* is a circumscribed set of symptoms that regularly appear whenever the intake of certain drugs is suddenly terminated. Popularly referred to as withdrawal, these syndromes vary somewhat depending on the drug under consideration. The public's picture of withdrawal is largely based on literary and mass media depictions of the *morphine abstinence syndrome* that results from heroin withdrawal. The *alcohol-barbiturate abstinence syndrome*, as we will see later, is quite different. Although such syndromes are as yet not fully understood, they appear to result from a latent hyperexcitability of the central nervous system brought about by continuous and excessive drug intake. Withholding the drug triggers nervous excitation and produces a number of painful and sometimes terrifying effects.

*Drug abuse*, finally, is less a physical or psychological concept than a sociocultural one. The use of drugs is considered sociopathic (abusive) when drug-seeking chronically interferes with social or vocational adjustment, or seriously jeopardizes health. The alcoholic may alienate his friends and co-workers and is repeatedly let go by employers; the heroin addict may steal from his family or send his wife out to whore in order to support his habit. Whether it is rooted in psychological dependence, physical dependence, or both, chronic drug-seeking tends to exclude other values in life, perhaps the most important of which is the maintenance of close interpersonal relationships.

The number of substances that can cause physical or psychological dependence are legion. Some of the more common ones are listed in Table 1.

Table 1

---

*Habituating and Addicting Drugs*

| DEPRESSANTS | STIMULANTS | PSYCHEDELICS |
|---|---|---|
| Alcohol | | |
| Narcotics: | Caffeine | Marijuana |
| Morphine | Nicotine | Psilocybin |
| Heroin | Cocaine | Mescaline |
| Synthetics (Methadone, | | LSD |
| Demerol, etc.) | Amphetamines: | |
| | Benzedrine | |
| Barbiturates: | Dexedrine | |
| Amytal | Methadrine | |
| Nembutal | | |
| Tranquilizers: | | |
| Equanil | | |
| Miltown | | |

---

Only the entries in the "Depressant" category are capable of producing physical dependence and, in this group, alcohol has by far the greatest potential for abuse. More people leave their jobs, experience marital break-ups, and wind up in mental hospitals as a result of alcohol abuse than of any drug. It is estimated that there are over five million alcohol addicts in the United States in addition to over six million heavy drinkers, persons who are habituated but who do not become addicted.

Addiction to alcohol is a slow insidious process taking months, even years, to develop. It often begins with a long period of moderate drinking in which alcohol is regularly relied upon to reduce personal inhibitions and alleviate mild anxiety. From this it passes into an intermediate phase involving secret drinking and occasional blackouts. In this phase, tolerance for alcohol increases markedly and an abstinence syndrome begins to develop. As the alcoholic progresses into the final phase of addiction, his intake of alcohol is heavy and relentless. He goes on drinking sprees lasting days, and in a pinch will drink anything, even rubbing alcohol. There is marked impairment of thought and gross disorientation, and with continued heavy drinking, irreversible brain damage occurs. Although there has been much research on alcoholism, little is known about why certain drinkers become addicted while others remain merely habituated.

Withdrawal from alcohol is an intense and potentially dangerous experience, one that optimally is carried out over a period of weeks. The withdrawal syndrome associated with alcohol addiction is referred to as the "DT's" (*delirium tremens*) and is characterized by tremors, confusion, epileptic-type seizures, and frightening hallucinations, experiences in which the addict sees and hears imaginary things. Thought once to be the result of excessive alcohol intake, the DT's are today recognized as the result of alcohol *deprivation* and technically included under the designation of alcohol-barbiturate abstinence syndrome.

Addiction to narcotics (morphine, heroin, and their synthetic derivatives) draws a great deal of public attention but is not as widespread nor as physically dangerous as addiction to alcohol. Although the use of narcotics seems to be on the rise, there are not nearly as many narcotic addicts as there are alcoholics. Narcotic addiction, furthermore, does not cause damage to the body; one can be addicted to heroin for years and subsequently withdrawn with no lasting physical effects (Fort, 1969, p. 99).

The pattern of addiction to heroin and the other morphine-like drugs differs from alcohol addiction in several ways. Firstly, the body adapts to narcotics in a relatively rapid fashion so that tolerance builds up fairly quickly; secondly, physical dependence usually develops after a much briefer time span; finally, the morphine abstinence syndrome differs qualitatively from the alcohol-barbiturate abstinence syndrome. Beginning with a running nose, teary eyes, and goose flesh, the morphine syndrome peaks at about forty hours after abstinence, culminating in severe muscular cramps, nauseau, vomiting, and hot and cold flashes. Unlike the alcohol-barbiturate syndrome, there are no hallucinations nor is there marked confusion or disorientation.

An example of narcotic withdrawal is vividly described by Barney Ross, once the light and welterweight champion of the world. Addicted to morphine during treatment for a World War II battle injury, Ross recounts his withdrawal at the now defunct Federal Narcotics Hospital at Lexington, Kentucky.

> The withdrawal gave me the miseries, because the limited amount of morphine wasn't enough to kill the cramps and the sweats. I soon learned where the expression "kick the habit" came from. When my drug quota was progressively cut down, I got spasms in the muscles of my arms and my legs actually kicked. . . .
>
> The morning went by. Then the afternoon. The cramps were getting worse. The diarrhea started now. It came so fast I had to twist my legs and roll over to try to hold it back. I had to vomit but there was no food in me so I gagged and choked till I forced out blood. My nose started to run and my eyes began to burn. I tried to lie down but the convulsions hit me and I began to bounce up and down on the bed like a rubber ball. (Ross and Abramson, 1957, p. 234)

Although withdrawal from narcotics is subjectively frightening and painful, it is not particularly dangerous; addicts can be withdrawn with relative safety. Narcotic treatment programs are concerned less with *getting* the heroin addict off drugs, than in *keeping* him off them.

The other major drug substances in the depressant category are the barbiturates. Commonly known as "red devils," "yellow jacks" and "downers,"
they produce relaxation and a sense of well-being at moderate dosages and
with infrequent use. With heavy and chronic use, they lead to physical
dependence, the latter indexed by an abstinence syndrome that is essentially
the same as that associated with alcoholism. Withdrawal from barbiturates,
like withdrawal from alcohol, is physically hazardous and, unless supervised by someone who has experience handling addicts, can be life-
threatening.

The greatest threat from barbiturates, however, is death from toxic
overdose. These drugs constitute the prime ingredients in sleeping pills
and thus represent one of the major ways by which people commit suicide.
They also are implicated in many accidental deaths. Heavy doses of barbiturates cause confusion, clouding of consciousness, and errors in time
perception; as one's ability to judge time is impaired, he may repeatedly
take barbiturates over brief time intervals, mistakenly thinking that hours
have passed. A lethal dose thus can be reached very quickly and without
awareness.

Of the substances in the other two major drug categories, stimulants
and psychedelics, none are capable of producing physical dependence,
although some of them still have a high potential for abuse. In the stimu-
lant group, amphetamines are the most likely candidates. Referred to as
"dex" (dexedrine), "bennies" (benzedrine), "speed" (methedrine), and
"uppers," amphetamines are used to produce elevations of mood and to
increase alertness. Amphetamines, like barbiturates, are easily available:
students use them to stay awake at night, athletes to improve their performance. Although amphetamines are not addictive, they are habituating,
and with continual use cause irritability, restlessness, insomnia, and tremor.
In heavy doses, they are capable of precipitating an "amphetamine psychosis," an intoxication syndrome characterized by anxiety, hallucinations,
and strong feelings of persecution.

In the psychedelic group, marijuana (pot, tea, grass, *cannabis*) has the
highest frequency of use but is least likely to be implicated in drug abuse.
Used in nineteenth century America as a remedy for coughs, migraine
headaches, and menstrual cramps, its primary use today is recreational.
Since marijuana is not a very potent drug, it does not seem able to provide
the satisfactions required by dependence-prone individuals. LSD, psilocy-
bin, mescaline, and hashish (a more powerful form of marijuana) have a
much greater potential for excitement and escape.

The ability of certain psychedelic drugs to produce strange sensory
experiences similar to hallucinations has led to their being labeled *hal-
lucinogens*. Perhaps the most well known of these is LSD, *lysergic acid
diethylamide*. LSD at times can produce exotic visual and auditory effects

as well as novel mystical experiences. However, at other times it may unexpectedly produce bizarre and frightening hallucinations. These contrasts are vividly described in the personal account of a journalist who reports the effects of an LSD episode. Of his more positive experiences, he writes:

> At times I beheld visions of dazzling beauty—visions so rapturous, so unearthly, that no artist will ever paint them. I lived in a paradise where the sky was a mass of jewels set in a background of shimmering aquamarine blue; where the clouds were apricot-colored; where the air was filled with liquid golden arrows, glittering fountains of iridescent bubbles, filigree lace of pearl and silver, sheaves of rainbow light—all constantly changing in color, design, texture and dimension so that each scene was more lovely than the one which preceded it. (Katz, 1953, p. 10)

These pleasant experiences were later followed by more frightening effects:

> I was conscious that my hands and body were vibrating as a prelude to a shrinking process. As I watched, my fingers grew shorter and telescoped into my hand, my hand telescoped into my arm. Suddenly, I was outside of myself looking down from above. My arms were now mere stumps as if they had been amputated near the shoulder. My legs were now shrinking and withering and my skin was coarse and scaly. I felt the pressure of space closing in on me from above, forcing my head—which was now double its normal size—out of shape. I fought against this awesome, macabre transformation by trying to stretch my arms and legs but found that I was powerless. Ultimately, all that was left of me was a hard, sickly, nauseous stone located in the lower left side of my abdomen, surrounded by a greeny-yellowish vapor which poured across the floor. (Katz, 1953, p. 46)

The mechanisms underlying these visual phenomena are still shrouded in mystery. Some scientists have speculated that LSD has a toxic effect on either the retina, the optical pathways, or the visual cortex. However, the specific effect that any drug produces remains largely a function of a person's expectations and his experience with drugs.

The topic of drug abuse, as we indicated earlier, is one of the perplexing issues of our time. It is a highly complex topic, having social, legal, and ethical ramifications. From a psychological point of view, it can be incorporated within both the intrapsychic and behovioristic models.

From an intrapsychic perspective, chronic drug-seeking is seen as a behavior pattern emerging in persons with a dependent personality structure. Such persons lack frustration tolerance and, when forced to face demands, depend upon others to provide them with nurturance and support. When other means of gratifying their needs fail, they turn to drugs. Viewed through an intrapsychic lens, drug abuse is a symptom of a malfunctioning personality.

If we approach drug-seeking as a conditioned habit, we find that several types of learning may be involved in its maintenance. Underlying most forms of habituation is the rewarding effect of the high associated with continued drug use. Positive reinforcement is capable of creating strong habitual craving for practically any drug substance. With the depressants, however, another potent factor is added—the actual or contemplated fear of abstinence. Once the user has experienced several withdrawals, a conditioned avoidance pattern develops. Combined with the drug's primary rewarding effect, it establishes drug-seeking as a durable and often immutable behavior pattern.

It is apparent that approaching drug abuse through either an intrapsychic *or* behavioristic perspective exclusively leaves us with an incomplete picture. Obviously it is important to consider the drug habit itself, regardless of why a person gets hooked; but because many individuals return to drugs long after they have been successfully withdrawn, it is necessary to examine personality factors as well. In the area of drugs, at least, the two models tend to complement one another.

SEXUAL DEVIATION

In most psychiatric texts, normal sexuality is depicted as sexual behavior whose *ultimate goal* is genital intercourse with a consenting adult. Within this definition, most sexual behavior as well as most forms of sexual foreplay are considered normal if, in fact, they eventually result in intercourse. If they come to represent ends in themselves, exclude intercourse, and grow to constitute the adult's major source of sexual gratification, they are likely to be labeled deviant.

There are, of course, difficulties with this definition. *Nymphomania* (hypersexuality in females) and its counterpart in males, *satyriasis*, are usually considered abnormal even though both typically involve heterosexual intercourse. Deviance in these instances is more a function of the frequency with which sexual stimulation is sought than of the form it takes. Behaviors that are labeled sexually deviant, moreover, change with the times and the culture. Homosexuality was not considered deviant in ancient Greece but is generally considered so today. Granted that definition difficulties exist, let us look at some of the more common forms of sexual behavior that are today regarded as deviant, categorizing them as deviations in *object choice* and deviations in *means of gratification.*

The types of objects (human and otherwise) with which people choose to engage in sex is virtually unlimited. Included in the category of abnormal object choice are such deviations as incest, zoophilia (sexual relations with animals), pedophilia (relations with young children), and a relatively rare perversion called necrophilia (relations with corpses). The most common form of deviance in this category, however, is homosexuality.

*Homosexuality* is the generic term used to denote sexual responsiveness to members of the same sex. Although more often used to describe erotic attachments among men, it also technically encompasses female–female, or *lesbian*, relationships. While homosexuality is practiced in a variety of ways, with mutual masturbation and oral–genital contact among the more common practices, it is not the activity itself that earns the label of deviance but the choice of sexual object. Many of the sexual behaviors found in homosexual partnerships are identical to those observed among hetero-sexuals.

Psychological explanations of homosexuality vary quite markedly al-though most place the origins of such behavior either in early traumatic events or early disturbances in the parent–child relationship. Some studies indicate that many homosexuals had been homosexually seduced while quite young, an experience that profoundly influenced the course of their future sexual development. While acknowledging that such occurrences may take place, Irving Bieber (1962), a psychoanalyst who has studied male homosexuality closely, argues that it is related more to an overly close relationship with a seductive mother than to youthful seductions. Mothers of this sort form intense psychological bonds with their children, preventing them from establishing masculine identities. Considerations such as these would lead one to predict that homosexuals invariably are conflicted and maladjusted. Nevertheless, in a study using standard per-sonality tests, Evelyn Hooker (1957) demonstrated that some homosexuals are relatively well adjusted. Under nonoppressive conditions, she contends, such individuals might function quite well in our society.

In recent years, there has been increasing interest regarding the homo-sexual's existence in our culture and the extent to which homosexual sub-cultures function to gratify deviant needs. One of the more interesting findings is that sexuality, per se, is not as important an element in homo-sexuality as was generally presumed. This is clearly seen in the following comment by a homosexual:

As far as I know, people who hang around with each other don't have affairs. The people who are friends don't sleep with each other. I can't tell you why that is, but they just don't. Unless you are married[1] you have sex with strangers mostly. I think if you have sex with a friend it will destroy the friendship. I think that in the inner mind we all respect

[1] A stable social and sexual relationship between two homosexuals is fre-quently referred to as "marriage."

high moral standards, and none of us want to feel low in the eyes of any-
body else. It's always easier to get along with your gay friends if there
has been no sex. (Leznoff and Westley, 1956, p. 258)

The homosexual subculture obviously offers more than the opportunity
to obtain sexual gratification. It provides the homosexual with a safe
setting in which his burdensome sense of difference can be shared.

Once an individual is identified as a homosexual, however, he is subject
to the ostracism that often accompanies deviant behavior. He then has
little recourse but to retreat even more into the gay world. There he may
be able to find some of the interpersonal comforts denied him by straights:

The thought that you are "gay" is always with you and you know it's
there even when other people don't. You also think to yourself that
certain of your mannerisms and your ways of expression are liable to
give you away. That means that there is always a certain amount of
strain. I don't say that it's a relief to get away from normal people, but
there isn't the liberty that you feel in a gay crowd. When I associate
with normal people I prefer very small groups of them. I don't like large
groups and I think I try to avoid them when I can. You know, the only
time when I really forget I'm gay is when I'm in a gay crowd. (Leznoff
and Westley, 1956, pp. 257–58)

Feelings and attitudes such as these have been changing in the past few
years. Backed by such organizations as The Mattachine Society, Gay Liberation Front, and the Daughters of Bilitis, homosexuals have been speaking out in defense of their right to be treated as human beings, and today
are a little less likely to seek anonymity.

Despite such changes, the homosexual's existence is fraught with difficulties and often filled with loneliness. Open acknowledgement of homosexuality typically leads to estrangement from the broader culture, while
passing results in clandestine sexual liaisons devoid of feeling and commitment. An example of the latter is seen in a study conducted by sociologist Laud Humphreys.

In *Tearoom Trade: Impersonal Sex in Public Places*, Humphreys describes the world of a subgroup of homosexuals who regularly frequent
public restrooms to perform fellatio (male oral–genital sex) on one
another. These restrooms, labeled "tearooms" in the slang of the homosexual subculture, provide convenient settings for instant, impersonal sex.
Situated in bus stations, public beaches, and in parks, they attract a variety
of clientele and provide the opportunity for sexual gratification while allowing the participants to preserve their anonymity. In the words of one of the
participants:

You go into the tearoom. You can pick up some really nice things in
there. Again, it is a matter of sex real quick; and if you like this kind,

fine—you've got it. You get one and he is done; and, before long, you've got another one. (Humphreys, 1970, p. 10)

By acting as a "watchqueen," a lookout in homosexual slang, Humphrey was able to chart patterns of homosexual fellatio in tearooms and to shed some insight into this common but rarely studied form of sexual deviance.

One of the more interesting findings that emerged from Humphrey's research concerned the characteristics of the people who frequent tearooms. Many hold respectable jobs, are masculine in appearance, and apparently are able to maintain masculine or bisexual identities. Perhaps the most striking finding was that 54 percent of the people studied were married and were living with their wives. A number of the married respondents in the study indicated a diminished frequency of intercourse with their wives. For these persons, however, an extra-marital affair or regular visits to a prostitute were religiously, ethically, or economically out of the question. Sex for them had to be quick, inexpensive, and impersonal. In Humphrey's words, "they want a form of orgasm-producing action that is less lonely than masturbation and less involving than a love relationship" (p. 18).

Whether homosexuality takes the form of impersonal liaisons of the sort just described or is characterized by an intimate, prolonged relationship as occurs in homosexual marriages, it represents deviance in the choice of *object*. Other patterns of sexual deviance are manifested in the atypical *means* by which some people achieve sexual gratification. Two prime examples of this are exhibitionism and voyeurism.

*Exhibitionism*, the exposure of one's genitals in public, is, along with homosexuality, one of the most widespread forms of sexual deviance. Frequently associated with doubts regarding masculinity, exhibitionistic behavior tends to be compulsive and driven. Exhibitionists report that they are gripped by recurrent urges to disrobe that they find difficult to ignore.

> I was out one day a little further from home than usual and resting against a railing, when opposite me at a groundfloor window I saw a young woman. She was standing just between two lace curtains and looking at me. Suddenly the thought flashed into my mind: "What if that girl should see me naked?" The idea was ridiculous, I knew, but my limbs began to tremble, and a cold sweat broke out over me. "What if I could not control myself, and I were to unfasten my clothes before her," was the next thought. I became torn with a panic . . . that I might expose myself. . . . (Raymond, 1946, p. 59)

Exhibitionism often acts as a prelude to orgasm, the successful completion of which functions to allay doubts regarding sexual competency. The exhibitionist parks his car near a place where he is sure to be seen (for example, a supermarket or bus stop), exposes himself, masturbates, and then retreats hastily. In such instances, the relation between exposure and proof of sexual adequacy is clearly evident.

*Voyeurism*, an excessive interest in viewing sexual organs (or the sexual act), is not as common as exhibitionism but still not rare. A common voyeuristic pattern is depicted in the behavior of the "Peeping Tom," a person for whom total sexual gratification lies in stealing a glimpse of a woman undressing or a couple making love. Witnessing sexual intercourse or the genitals of others provides, in itself, sufficient stimulation for complete sexual satisfaction. Although whole neighborhoods sometimes panic when they suspect that such persons are on the prowl, their fears are groundless. Peeping Toms tend to be quite fearful of others, which is perhaps the reason they resort to secretive, solitary means of satisfying their sexual needs.

Voyeuristic behavior is of more than passing interest since in a less extreme form it exists as a common phenomenon in our culture. Voyeuristic tendencies are pandered to in girlie magazines, "X"-rated motion pictures, and thousands upon thousands of advertisements in which the human body is provocatively displayed. Such appeals rely upon the tendency of visual stimuli to act as sexual stimulants. The extreme case, of course, is pornography.

Of specific interest in the context of our current discussion is the extent to which exposure to pornography is responsible for sexually deviant acts. Many high ranking government officials, including J. Edgar Hoover, have publicly declared that pornography not only precipitates sexual offenses (exhibitionism, voyeurism, rape, and so on) but a host of nonsexual crimes as well. The belief that exposure to explicit sexual material causes sex crimes is apparently shared by the general public. In a recent survey of public attitudes toward erotica (Abelson *et al.*, 1970) 56 percent of the respondents answered "Yes" to "Sexual materials lead to a breakdown of morals," and 49 percent responded in the same way to "Sexual materials lead people to commit rape."

In attempting to study more generally how erotica affects behavior, The President's Commission on Obscenity and Pornography (1970) addressed itself to the relation between sexual deviance and exposure to pornography. One avenue of investigation led them to study what had taken place in Denmark where the distribution of pornographic material had been legalized in 1967, a year in which sales of erotica, not surprisingly, peaked. The Commission selected a study in which sexual offenses in Copenhagen were tabulated during the twelve year period from 1958 to 1969. The study thus encompassed the year in which pornographic sales were at their highest.

The results of the study are given in Table 2. As can be seen, there

## Table 2

*Number and Percent Change in Sex Crimes Reported to
Copenhagen Police, by Offense Category, 1958–1969*

| OFFENSE CATEGORY | 1958 | 1969 | % CHANGE |
|---|---|---|---|
| *Heterosexual offenses* | *846* | *330* | *-61.0* |
| Rape (including attempts) | 52 | 27 | -48.1 |
| Intercourse on threat of violence or by fraud, etc. | 11 | 8 | -37.5 |
| Unlawful interference short of rape with adult women | 100 | 52 | -48.0 |
| Unlawful interference short of rape with minor girls | 249 | 87 | -65.1 |
| Coitus with minors | 30 | 19 | -57.9 |
| Exhibitionism | 264 | 104 | -60.6 |
| Peeping | 87 | 20 | -77.0 |
| Verbal indecency | 53 | 13 | -32.5 |
| *Homosexual offenses* | *128* | *28* | *-78.1* |

From *The Report of the Commission on Obscenity and Pornography.* (Ben-Veniste, 1970, p. 274)

was a decrease in every category of sexual offense listed, with particularly large decreases noted in "Exhibitionism," "Peeping," and "Homosexuality." Further study demonstrated that these changes could not be attributed to changes in law enforcement practices, police data collection, or the public's willingness to report such offenses.

Additional investigation by the Commission focused on American sex offenders. Their findings revealed that such offenders were no more likely than other adults to engage in sexual behavior during or following exposure to erotica. An examination of the background of sexual deviants indicated that as children these individuals were exposed to *less* rather than more erotica than normals. The early environment of sex offenders tended to be characterized as sexually repressive, with the parents manifesting indifferent or punitive reactions to the child's sexual curiosity. The Commission concluded: "Extensive empirical investigation . . . provides no evidence that exposure to or use of explicit sexual materials play a significant role in the causation of social or individual harms such as crime, delinquency, sexual or non-sexual deviancy, or severe emotional disturbances" (p. 58).

While attitudes toward sexual deviance in America are changing, a great deal of ambivalence and confusion remain. Hopefully, some of the myths regarding sexual deviance will be exploded as more information about deviant behavior and deviant subcultures is made available. It may be that someday we will focus not on deviant sexual behaviors, per se, but on the deviant ways in which people deal with one another.

The sociopathic disturbances, in sum, consist of an assortment of striking and puzzling disorders. Not only are they difficult to treat but often they prove difficult to diagnose. Some workers in the field argue that sociopathy as a clinical entity does not really exist and that a diagnosis of sociopathy is only a "wastebasket" diagnosis for patients who cannot be categorized as either neurotic or psychotic. Whatever the merit of this argument, it does not detract from the fact that there are people who are chronically asocial, and whose relations with others tend to be outside the bounds normally dictated by social norms. Such asocial patterns of behavior result in continuing difficulties with friends and relatives, if not with the law, and ultimately bring sociopathic individuals to the attention of psychologists and psychiatrists.

## Psychotic Disorders

Psychoses are characterized by severe disruption in personal and social functioning as well as by bizarre behavior. They are the disorders most frequently associated with the phrase "out of touch with reality," a shorthand way of describing disturbances in the patient's thought processes. As his cognitive functions become disrupted, the patient's school, job, and family functions also deteriorate and hospitalization is frequently required.

The presence of psychosis is generally indicated by some combination of the following factors·

> Disordered language and thought
> Disturbed affect
> Social withdrawal
> Delusions
> Hallucinations

At least one and usually several of these factors is associated with each psychotic syndrome.

*Disturbances in language and thought* are reflected in the unconventional ways by which a psychotic patient orders his world. This is most apparent in the way he communicates. At times, the patient may be coherent but illogical, coming up with statements such as "My bed is a space ship," or "My body is dead." At other times, the words themselves are vague and ambiguous. This often results from the patient's use of *neologisms*, new expressions formed by combining elements of different words (*neo*=new, *logos*=*word*). A psychotic patient's association of benzine and turpentine may emerge in the neologistic "terpenzine," cruel orderlies as "cruelies." Disordered language processes, finally, are reflected in the patient's concrete or tangential ways of responding to simple questions. A psychotic is likely to reply to the inquiry, "How do you feel?" with a detailed description of his tactile skills. A hospitalized schizophrenic, in response to the author's question, "What brought you to the hospital?" replied in utmost seriousness: "A 1965 Plymouth."

*Disturbed affect* refers to inappropriate emotional responses and is manifested in a variety of ways. The patient's emotional reactions, for one, may be incongruous. He laughs in response to sad tidings and cries when offered good news. Emotional reactions in psychosis also are often disproportionately intense. When the patient is happy, he is overjoyed beyond his wildest dreams; when he is sad, he reaches the depths of despair. All of this is particularly striking since his responses do not seem to have any objective basis. Finally, the patient's affect may be *blunted*. In such cases, the psychotic seems unable to conjure up any emotional response—positive or negative.

*Social withdrawal* refers to self-initiated behavior resulting in isolation from other human beings. The patient retreats into a psychological shell, and is aloof, unresponsive, and oblivious to his surroundings. In extreme cases, social withdrawal leads to *mutism* (refusal to speak) and *regression* (acting in infantile ways). Under such conditions, the patient may eat with his fingers, suck his thumb, have temper tantrums, and even smear feces.

*Delusions* are false beliefs that the patient maintains in the face of overwhelming contradictory evidence. Among the various types of delusions are found delusions of grandeur and delusions of persecution. In the former, the patient believes he has extraordinary skills or is a great figure; such delusions generate the well-worn jokes about mental patients who believe themselves to be Napoleon. Delusions of persecution center about the patient's belief that another person or group of persons plan to do him harm. In these delusions, plots and conspiracies form the backdrop for all sorts of imagined persecutions. These as well as other types of delusions are discussed in more detail later on.

*Hallucinations* refer to sensory experiences for which there are no apparent stimuli. The patient hears voices or noises where there is silence (auditory hallucinations), and sees things where there is nothing to be seen (visual hallucinations). Auditory hallucinations often occur as voices; the patient hears people accusing, praising, or condemning him. Nonverbal sounds such as rustling, mumuring, or laughter, however, also are common.

Visual hallucinations are as variable as the auditory type, but commonly involve human figures. Depending on the particular case, such figures may be experienced as distinct, shadowy, or faceless. Hallucinating patients also report seeing objects ranging from pyramids to palm trees to talking animals. Whereas in the early stages of a psychotic episode patients will regard these sensations as figments of their imaginations, they eventually come to believe that they are very real.

It might be wise to point out before continuing that experiences similar to those just described are not as rare as one might think. People often break into smiles when the situation seems to call for tears, harbor strong beliefs that others have it in for them, or hear mysterious footsteps behind them in dark alleys and swear that they are real. Experiences such as these, even though they represent transient distortions of reality, are not in and by themselves indicative of psychosis. It is when these experiences occur repeatedly and begin interfering with social obligations that a diagnosis of psychosis is apt to be made. Bearing this in mind, we turn to the specific syndromes of psychosis as represented by depression, mania and schizophrenia.

### DEPRESSION

The major characteristics of psychotic depression are overwhelming despair, marked slowdown of physical and mental processes, and feelings of guilt. These are often accompanied by a variety of secondary symptoms such as loss of appetite, insomnia, and frequent weeping. The symptom picture, in a general way, approximates that seen in states of bereavement. In psychotic depression, however, there typically has been no immediate death among family or friends, and where there has been a death, the depression lasts far beyond the normal mourning period.

As a depression develops, mental apathy is joined by physical apathy. A slowdown, or retardation, in bodily movements takes place, and the patient is unable to initiate activities or keep on the go. The combined physical and mental exhaustion characteristic of psychotic depression is clearly depicted in the report of a nurse who personally endured such an experience:

> I was seized with an unspeakable physical weariness. There was a tired feeling in the muscles unlike anything I had ever experienced. A peculiar sensation appeared to travel up my spine to my brain. I had an indescribable nervous feeling. . . . My nights were sleepless. I lay with dry, staring eyes gazing into space. I had a fear that some terrible calamity was about to happen. I grew afraid to be left alone. The most trivial duty became a formidable task. Finally mental and physical exercises became impossible; the tired muscles refused to respond; my "thinking apparatus" refused to work; ambition was gone. My general feeling might be summed up in the familiar saying, "What's the use." I had tried so hard to make something of myself, but the struggle seemed useless. Life seemed utterly futile. (Reid, 1910, pp. 612–13)

As feelings of hopelessness mount, delusions of worthlessness develop.

Such delusions represent feelings of guilt and sinfulness carried to extreme proportions. Believing he has sinned beyond redemption, the patient concludes that his misery (and sometimes the miseries of the world) is punishment for his transgressions. He maintains this position in the face of carefully measured arguments by loved ones who try to persuade him that such beliefs are unwarranted.

Delusions of worthlessness quite often lead to thoughts of suicide. In the eyes of the patient, this final act of desperation seems to offer the only solution for his unending torment.

> For some inscrutable reason, perhaps because I had committed "the unforgivable sin" or just because I was such an appalling sinner, the worst man who ever existed, I had been chosen to go alive through the portals of Hell in an ordinary English lunatic asylum. . . . [My wife] was the only person to whom I dared confide my horrors, and I tried hard to show [her] my train of reasoning. Roughly it was that I was sort of opposite of Jesus Christ. Satan's job had been to catch a man, get him to sell his soul to him completely and utterly, like Faust, and then take him down into the pit. That was a sort of necessary counterweight to the resurrection of Jesus. . . . But if I could only kill myself . . . at least I would get out of eternal torture and achieve the oblivion and nothingness for which my soul craved. I did in fact make three attempts at suicide, the most serious of which was when I tore myself from my attendant and threw myself in front of a car, with my poor wife, who was visiting me, looking on. (Custance, 1952, pp. 66–67)

Delusions of worthlessness, like most delusions, are based on irrational premises; however, they contain an internal logic that is difficult to dispute. If, as the above example demonstrates, the premise of worthlessness is accepted, then suicide as the ultimate form of self-punishment is not an illogical consequence.

Psychotic depression, in sum, consists of a number of different symptoms, namely guilt feelings, false beliefs, depressed affect, and thoughts of suicide. With regard to the major signs of psychosis presented earlier, it is disturbance in affect (severe depression) and delusions (of worthlessness) that predominate.

## MANIA

The behaviors associated with mania seem the opposite of those seen in depression. Rather than being despondent, the manic patient is elated, confident, and excitable; instead of feeling physically exhausted and worn out, he is tireless and full of energy. Patients suffering from a manic psychosis are constantly joking, laughing, and making impromptu speeches on all sorts of unconventional topics.

Despite an outward air of exuberance, the manic patient is far from happy or content. A close examination reveals his hyperactivity to be a cover-up for sustained tension. He is continually on the move not because he wants to be but because he is driven to it. In some cases, patients drive themselves to such a feverish pitch that they collapse from exhaustion.

Manic and depressive psychoses are similar in that both involve delusions as well as extremes in affect, or mood. However, the character of the delusions in each disturbance differs as markedly as the quality of the mood changes. In manic disturbances, the patient's delusions center about power and greatness as contrasted with the depressed patient's delusions of worthlessness. The manic patient suffers from grandiose delusions.

The grandiose delusions of the manic patient convince him that he is capable of anything. As a result, faith healing, political coups, or great sexual conquests are now within his reach. The patient, by dint of the fact that he is delusional, fails to recognize such beliefs for what they truly are—expressions of his internal fantasies. Believing his new-found capabilities to be real, he is liable to act upon them. In the following case study, a state of maximal excitement, combined with early signs of a grandiose delusion, indicates the presence of a manic psychosis.

> A thirty-five-year old biochemist was brought to the clinic by his frightened wife. . . . He entered the ward in high spirits, went about greeting the patients, insisted that the place was "swell," and made quick puns on the names of doctors to whom he was introduced. . . .
>
> When his wife had left, the patient . . . bounded down the hall, threw his medication on the floor, leaped on a window ledge and dared anyone to get him down. When he was put in a room alone where he could be free, he promptly dismantled the bed, pounded on the walls, yelled and sang. He made a sudden sally into the hall and did a kind of hula-hula dance before he could be returned to his room. . . .
>
> The following morning, after almost no sleep, the patient was more noisy and energetic than ever. He smashed the overhead light with his shoes and ripped off the window guard. He tore up several hospital gowns, draped himself in a loin cloth made of their fragments, said he was Tarzan, and gave wild jungle cries to prove it. "I've tasted tiger's blood!" he roared. "I'm a success and I'm the man for my boss's job. I've made a killing and this time I will keep on going." He made amorous remarks to the nurses, accused them of flirting with him, and announced loudly, "At the present time I am not married; but my body is not for sale, regardless of the price." (Cameron and Margaret, 1951, p. 332)

The hyperactivity of manic patients, coupled with their repeated grandiose claims, leads others to regard them as quite deranged. It is not surprising that the expression "maniac" derives from the term "mania."

The similarities between mania and depression have led some clinicians to believe that the two disorders are actually different phases of a single disturbance. Biologically oriented clinicians argue that an organic defect underlies both and that metabolic changes dictate which behavior will dominate at any particular time. Those of a more psychological persuasion argue that manic behavior is a reaction to, or a denial of, depressive feelings: the patient's response is to keep "on the move," psychologically and physically, in order to defend against the depression that he feels is imminent. Despite years of clinical and laboratory investigation, this issue remains unresolved.

SCHIZOPHRENIA

All the behavioral indications of psychosis that were listed earlier are likely to appear in schizophrenia. The schizophrenic often withdraws from social contact for extended periods of time and demonstrates abnormal emotional responses, often in the form of "blunted affect." But the disorder is primarily identified by bizarre deviations in thought and perception. For this reason we will concentrate on disturbed language, delusions, and hallucinations.

Disturbed language functions in schizophrenia often are first detected by subtle slips in the patient's speech—a word occasionally inserted into a sentence where it does not belong, or an irrelevant phrase disrupting an otherwise consistent conversation. As such events become more frequent they interfere with the patient's ability to communicate. An extreme example is seen in the following interview between a schizophrenic patient and his doctor:

> DOCTOR: What are you talking about?
> ROBERT: I've been lured, I've been lured time and time again. I've been lured by mobs and lured by money to build space. They talk about pleasure principle, pleasure purpose, it's merely false sex.
> DOCTOR: What do you mean?
> ROBERT: I know what I'm doing. I'm living out my grandfather's life. They had to tell me, my mother went. America sees its own heirs.
> DOCTOR: Does God talk to you?
> ROBERT: No, I don't get voices. I just used that for a sex point.
> DOCTOR: Do you see some particular pattern for the world?
> ROBERT: It's immaterial. I don't say I can't use the moon. God made the moon so let it have it. I'm like a psychiatrist and I'm trying to help my mother.
> DOCTOR: What's wrong with her?
> ROBERT: I've got intuition. She doesn't seem to want to be a father. If she'd show me a written statement I'll be the priest. (Zax and Stricker, 1963, p. 65)

This transcription clearly demonstrates why psychotherapy with schizophrenics is such a long and arduous process.

Careful examination of the schizophrenic's bizarre responses often reveals that they derive from loosened associations. Whereas most people would, through normal associative processes, come up with a similar response for the missing word in "red, white, and ———, many schizophrenics would not. The associative link that leads to a correct response in this situation has, in the schizophrenic's case, gone awry. Thus we have the case of the schizophrenic patient who, in the midst of complaining about the hospital's laundry service, began to expound on Chinese communism. The word "Chinese" formed the associative link that led from laundry to communism.

The irrational conclusions that result from the schizophrenic's associations are depicted in an example provided by Joseph Church, a psychologist writing on pathological language. Church describes a schizophrenic who attributed powers to him because of a series of remote associations made to the author's name:

> From the beginning, ( the patient) attributed rather heroic qualities to the author, perhaps because of the ecclesiastic overtones of his name. In addition, however, *Church* both begins and ends with *ch*, which are the third and eighth letters of the alphabet; and so the word can be written 38UR38. . . . Since 38UR is *ur* flanked by two 38's, it can also be rendered UR238, which was close enough to the symbol for uranium to convince (the patient) that the author was imbued with atomic energy. And since *Church* contains two h's, it contains H², or heavy hydrogen, or the makings of a hydrogen bomb as well. (1961, p. 159)

Remote associations of this sort, coupled with the development of delusions and hallucinations, are what is meant by "loss of reality contact."

Delusions, it will be recalled, are false beliefs that the patient clings to tenaciously and ultimately comes to accept as reality. Delusions in schizophrenia may take various forms, such as beliefs that strange things are taking place in the body (somatic delusions) or beliefs that one's behavior is being controlled by alien forces (delusions of influence). Among the more common delusions are those of persecution and grandeur described earlier. Schizophrenic disturbances in which persecutory and/or grandiose delusions are prominent are referred to as *paranoid schizophrenia.*

The topic of delusions has been the subject of many investigations. Milton Rokeach, a social scientist interested in the formation and maintenance of belief systems, conducted a study that focused upon the resistance of delusional beliefs to change. In *The Three Christs of Ypsilanti* (1964), Rokeach tells of three different paranoid patients, each of whom suffered from grandiose delusions and insisted that he was Jesus Christ. What makes this study so fascinating is that all were in the same hospital at the same time. Rokeach brought the three together on a regular basis for many months to see if their beliefs would change upon being continually confronted with the ultimate paradox—other human beings claiming the same identity.

In their early meetings the three Christs had daily arguments over their identities and resorted to denial when asked to explain the claims of the others. One explained away the interpersonal discrepancy by declaring that the other two were not really alive. As the months progressed the arguments died down. Nevertheless, the confrontations failed to alter their delusions. One patient called Rex, who claimed that his true name was *Dr. Domino Dominorum et Rex Rexarum, Simplis Christianus Pueris Mentalis Doktor* (Latin for "Lord of Lords, and King of Kings, Simple Christian Boy Psychiatrist") did change his name during the course of the study to Dr. R. I. Dung. His new name, however, did not represent a change of identity but rather an attempt to make his Christ identity impervious to attack by keeping it hidden from public view.

Grandiose schizophrenics often believe that they have extraordinary skills or phenomenal powers. The following patient felt he could control others by means of a powerful radar beam lodged in his body:

> My radar beam was a source of delight to me. Not only did it not diminish, but I found that I could exercise a certain control over it; I was able to summon it at will or to extinguish it. It had become very useful to me on the ward. I could repel attendants or patients at will. All that was necessary was to recognize the central source of heat in my solar plexus and move it into my eyes, stare angrily at my enemy and he would become pale, frightened and usually leave. Since the source of power was definitely located inside me, in my chest, it must obviously come from the sun. Solar power, solar plexus. For this reason, whenever I was not engaged in some routine—eating, visiting the latrine, having my bandages changed—I gazed at the sun, absorbing its light and warmth. (Peters, 1949, pp. 143–44)

The interesting derivation of solar power from solar plexus is, incidentally, another example of the loosened associations discussed earlier.

Persecutory delusions, as the name implies, involve beliefs centering on themes of victimization. The schizophrenic believes that others wish to torment him or do him harm. The case study in the beginning pages of this book in which a college girl believed her actions to be monitored by a powerful group of professors illustrates this type of delusion. Schizophrenics very often intertwine cultural agencies, such as the FBI, the CIA, and the Bell Telephone Company into their intricate belief systems. Some try to escape their tormentors by fleeing to other towns only to find that they have been pursued and located with exacting precision.

In *Operators and Things*, a young woman, after recovery from a psychotic episode, writes of her persecution by a group of devilish tormentors called "Operators." Some of these, charged with the task of torturing Things (victims), were referred to as "Hook Operators."

> Whenever I think of the Hook Operators now, I see a picture of a man with a hook stuck in his back. The hook is attached to a rope and the rope hangs from the ceiling. At the end of the rope, unable to get his feet on solid ground, the man dangles in the air, his face distorted in agony, his arms and legs thrashing about violently.
>
> Behind him stands the Hook Operator. Having operated his hook successfully, the Hook Operator stands by with his other instruments, the knife and the hatchet. (O'Brien, 1958, p. 16)

In another passage, the writer tries to figure out a way to elude her persecutors who are able to read minds and who persistently accompany her in everything she does:

> A thought occurred to me. "Over what distance can an Operator influence the mind of a Thing?"
>
> "About two and a half city blocks. Not all Operators can extend that far though. Some of them can't extend beyond twenty feet. . . ."
>
> If I could get a two-block distance from all Operators, I thought my mind would have peace and might heal and close. Obviously, the Operators had opened my mind wide so that any Operator could tune in. What I needed to carry out my plan was money. If I went home, I could draw out what money I had in the bank and buy a small house with a lot of land around it. (O'Brien pp. 44–45)

Her attempts to escape were continually foiled since her primary means of transportation, Greyhound buses, were driven by Operators:

> I learned that the Greyhound Bus Company was a favorite vehicle of transport for Operators.
>
> "Greyhound is controlled by Operators. . . . The driver of a Greyhound bus is always an Operator, licensed as an Operator cop, a Shield" (O'Brien, p. 41).

Not all schizophrenic delusions are as sharply articulated as this one. The persecutory agents in many cases are only vaguely perceived and cannot be identified. When the schizophrenic is questioned as to who is trying to harm, poison, or kill him, he simply replies, "They."

Psychotic hallucinations, or persistent false perceptions, appear much more frequently in schizophrenic disturbances than in depression or mania. By far the most common type of hallucination is auditory. But whether it is auditory or visual, an hallucination tends to be a perplexing, often frightening, experience. It is a figment of one's imagination mistaken for reality.

*Auditory hallucinations* often are preceded by a period in which the patient states that he hears his thoughts aloud. This becomes an hallucination when he no longer makes this distinction and insists that he hears actual voices. In the following excerpt, a woman journalist writes of her experiences as she prepared to go to sleep.

> My head had scarcely touched the pillow when a man's voice—a very pleasant baritone voice—proceeding apparently from the large armchair by the fireplace, asked clearly and aloud—"Are you awake?"
>
> I raised myself on my left elbow, and facing the direction whence the voice came, and feeling suddenly no longer tired, but brisk and most alert, I answered—"Yes, wide awake. Who are you?" . . .
>
> The "voice" ignored my question and went on—"Are you not the author of (*Beyond the Occult*)?" . . . .
>
> "Yes!" I exclaimed in surprise. "But how can you possibly know of it? It was never published." (Anon., 1932a, p. 7)

In a later episode, the voice commanded her to kneel down, pray, and then strip. After complying, she was told that a fiend had entered her body and that she would bear a "fiend-child." This sent her into a state of frenzy and despair. Fortunately for this patient, her hallucinatory episode took place in the twentieth century. Had she lived in the Middle Ages, she probably would have been charged with consorting with the devil and executed at the stake.

In *visual hallucinations* fantasy once again is mistaken for reality. Visual experiences of this sort sometimes occur as isolated incidents. However, at other times they form essential elements of complex delusional schemes, as in the following episode described in *Operators and Things*. The author awoke one morning to find three strange figures standing at the edge of her bed telling her that she had been selected for an important experiment:

> When I awoke they were standing at the foot of my bed looking like soft fuzzy ghosts. I tried feeling the bedclothes. The sensation of feeling was sharp. I was awake and this was real. . . .
>
> "I am Burt," said the elderly man. He seemed concerned but in a dead, resigned sort of way, a man who had lived long with order and system and who was having difficulty adjusting to the role of master of ceremonies at a holocaust.
>
> "And this is Nicky." The boy smiled a wide, sunny smile.
>
> Burt explained. I could see why he had been chosen spokesman. What he had to say, he said clearly and in a few words. I had been selected for participation in an experiment. He hoped I would be co-

operative; lack of cooperation on my part would make matters difficult for them and for myself. They were Operators, the three of them. There were Operators everywhere in the world although they rarely were seen or heard. My seeing and hearing them was, unfortunately, a necessary part of the experiment. (O'Brien, 1958, pp. 31–32)

Although in this example the hallucinations took human form, schizophrenics also report seeing strange animals, shadowy ghost-like figures, and a wide variety of inanimate objects. As with auditory hallucinations, the content of visual hallucinations is limited only by the range of one's memory and imagination.

The psychotic syndromes, in sum, represent relatively serious disturbances characterized by intense mood swings and disruptions in cognition and perception. Very often we see the creation of a fantasy world accompanied by a breakdown in social functioning. Although there are some persons who can continue to meet job and family responsibilities while experiencing a psychosis, most have to be hospitalized.

The different syndromes that we have described in this chapter represent only a partial list of all the functional disturbances. Although major representatives of each of the primary categories (neurosis, sociopathy, and psychosis) were described, there exist subcategories within subcategories. The latest *Diagnostic and Statistical Manual of Mental Disorders* (American Psychiatric Association, 1968), for example, lists no less than fourteen varieties of schizophrenia. Included are schizoaffective schizophrenia (a form of schizophrenia accompanied by intense mood swings), childhood schizophrenia, paranoid schizophrenia, and chronic undifferentiated schizophrenia, the last a catchall diagnosis for patients who do not fit into any of the other thirteen categories.

The question of whether this classification scheme has any utility insofar as our current understanding of psychopathology is concerned is debatable. The reliability of psychiatric diagnosis, for one, is very weak. Studies have shown that while most clinicians have little trouble distinguishing between the major classifications (psychosis vs. neurosis, schizophrenia vs. depression, and so on), they have difficulty accurately assigning psychiatric patients to specific diagnostic categories. The reasons for this are complex, but a major one seems to be that the classical syndromes described in textbooks are more the exception than the rule. Most psychiatric patients display a variety of symptoms, many of which cut across different categories. The schizophrenic often displays obsessive–compulsive symptoms, the drug abuser may hallucinate, and the depressed psychotic may also be an alcoholic.

Nevertheless, the APA classification system tends to persist if for no other reason than that clinicians have not been able to come up with any other widely acceptable scheme. It thus is important to always bear in mind that symptoms are merely abstractions and to date represent little more than convenient devices for grouping people together. Behind every set of symptoms is a troubled human being with his own unique set of fears and failings and his own unique way of calling out for help. This is saliently reflected in Rokeach's reflections on his work with the Three Christs of Ypsilanti:

> In the course of our study we learned many things. In addition to those already discussed we have also learned: that if we are patient long enough, the apparent incoherence of psychotic utterance and behavior becomes increasingly more understandable; that psychosis is a far cry from the happy state some make it out to be; that it may sometimes represent the best terms a person can come to with life; that psychotics, having good reason to flee human companionship, nevertheless crave it. (1964, p. 331)

# Perspectives on Schizophrenia

## chapter three

Schizophrenia, characterized by complex and unusual symptoms, is perhaps the most difficult of all psychiatric syndromes for the public to understand. However, the delusions, hallucinations, and obscure speech patterns of the schizophrenic puzzle not only the layman but the clinician and researcher as well. The result has been the development of a vast body of theoretical and empirical literature on this one topic alone; it is therefore possible to use schizophrenia for an in-depth examination of the ways scientists approach pathological phenomena.

The literature on schizophrenia subsumes many different types of formulations. Some are broad, theoretical hypotheses whose primary function is to generate new ideas and mark off areas where further investigation might prove profitable. The value of such formulations often lies in their ability to reconcile a wide variety of clinical observations. Other formulations tend to be more limited in scope. Designed to explain only a restricted range of clinical phenomena, they are more likely to generate precise and quantifiable hypotheses.

In this chapter, samples of both emphases are explored. This not only allows us to delve more deeply into the disorder's distinctive features, but also provides a better picture of the types of activities in which psychologists and other social scientists are currently engaged. The first half of the chapter is devoted to a consideration of psychological formulations; the second half examines the biological and sociological perspectives.

## The Psychological Perspective

Most approaches to the study of schizophrenia phrased in psychological terms tend to focus either on the origins of the disturbance or on its symptoms. Formulations dealing with *origins* are usually couched in historical terms and attempt to uncover crucial factors predating the onset of the disorder; those dealing with symptoms tend to be relatively ahistorical, focusing on the *processes* that underlie the patient's current behavior. In this section we will look at several representatives of each approach.

### ORIGINS OF SCHIZOPHRENIA

Psychological formulations of schizophrenia that attempt to deal with questions of etiology, or origins, tend to emphasize the social antecedents of the disorder. Examples of this emphasis are the process-reactive dichotomy, the regression hypothesis, and the double-bind hypothesis. All three attempt to explain through past events why certain persons are more likely than others to become schizophrenic.

**The process-reactive dichotomy.** The severity of schizophrenia has led many clinicians to conclude that only a basic disruption in a patient's very early relationships could account for his bizarre behavior. This conclusion has resulted in a large number of studies in which the premorbid (pre-illness) status of the schizophrenic has been compared with that of normals. In such studies, schizophrenia has typically been treated as a homogeneous disease entity, as a disorder in which all patients are considered more or less clinical equals. A relatively recent distinction, the process-reactive dichotomy, challenges this assumption.

This distinction defines two major forms of schizophrenia: "process" schizophrenia and "reactive" schizophrenia. The essential difference between the two is that in the former, schizophrenic behavior appears to be the end result of a longterm *process* of deterioration, while in the latter the disorder seems more an extreme *reaction* to situational stress. Process schizophrenia is associated with a history of chronic maladjustment, a slow and insidious onset of symptoms, and poor prognosis for recovery. Reactive schizophrenia, in contrast, is characterized by relatively good premorbid adjustment, sudden onset, and a favorable recovery pattern.

Concern with this rather striking dichotomy has led many investigators to conclude that process schizophrenia results from a genetic defect while reactive schizophrenia stems from psychological factors. Noted authorities in the area, however, have surveyed the available evidence and concluded that there is little support for this assertion. Becker (1959), for example, feels that process and reactive schizophrenia simply represent end points on a continuum of personality organization. Herron (1962) concurs, stating, "There does not appear to be any significant evidence to support the contention of a process-organic versus a reactive-psychogenic formulation of schizophrenic etiology" (p. 341). Although there is still some disagreement as to whether process and reactive patients vary on an organicity dimension, the fact nevertheless remains that the two groups are unmistakably different. Furthermore, preliminary findings indicate that members of each group seem to have different types of relationships with their parents, a finding of major etiological significance.

One of the first investigations aimed at uncovering early familial differences between process and reactive schizophrenics was conducted by Jessie Harris, Jr. (1957). By employing a perceptual distortion task, Harris sought to discover whether the two groups differed in their response to maternal stimuli. The rationale underlying his investigation resulted from earlier studies in which perceptual distortion occurred as a response to stimuli bearing strong emotional connotations. In the classic study in this area, Bruner and Goodman (1947) demonstrated that poor children tended to make errors in estimating the size of coins of different monetary values. Extrapolating to the present study, Harris reasoned that process and reactive schizophrenics would differ in their size estimations of pictures containing maternal cues if, in fact, they were differentially sensitive to such stimuli.

To test this hypothesis, Harris presented a series of pictures of different types of mother-child interactions to twenty-five hospitalized schizophrenics and twenty-five hospitalized normals (medical and surgical patients). Figure 5 illustrates the stimuli used. The first scene (tree and bush) and sixth scene (square) were included as control stimuli. Subjects were briefly exposed to each of the stimuli separately projected on a screen and then asked to estimate their size from memory. They did this by adjusting a slide carriage until the picture on the screen was judged to be the same size as the standard. The subject's adjustments were noted, and scored as deviations (in percentage) from the standard.

The results are presented in two ways. Figure 6a compares the performance of the total schizophrenic group with the normal group. As can be seen, there is little difference between the two. Figure 6b shows the schizophrenic sample subdivided into its process and reactive components. Differences that were earlier masked are now clearly apparent.

Statistical tests indicate, furthermore, that the process and reactive groups differ significantly on all the stimuli except for the square. The

1. Neutral
3. Acceptance
5. Overprotection

2. Dominance
4. Ignoring
6. Square

FIGURE 5.  Maternal interaction stimuli. After Harris (1957, p. 654).

only puzzling finding concerns the response of the different subjects to the first stimulus (tree-bush). The subjects obviously did not regard this stimulus as neutral. The authors suggest that the "large-tree–little-bush" may have symbolically represented a parent-child configuration for many subjects and thus had an opposite effect than intended.

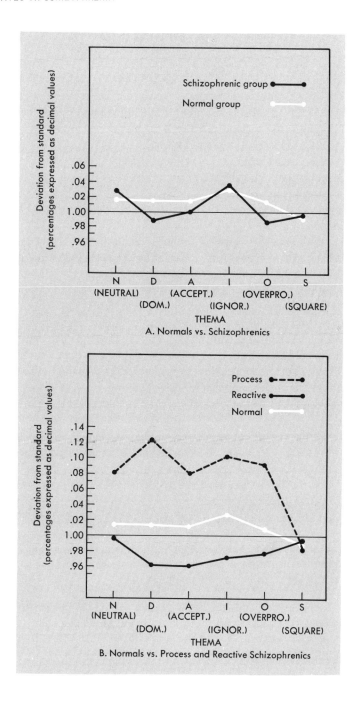

FIGURE 6. Size estimations of maternal interaction stimuli. From Harris (1957, pp. 659–60).

The Harris study, along with many other studies, tends to implicate the mother of the schizophrenic. The *schizophrenogenic* (schizophrenia-producing) mother, accordingly, has been the focus of a great many investigations aimed at clarifying the precise character of the schizophrenic's early familial relationships. Despite the abundance of data generated over the years, results have been disappointing. Depending on the study, mothers of schizophrenics have been portrayed as highly restrictive, overly protective, rejecting, aloof, and over-involved. In one study comparing 100 mothers of schizophrenic males with a control group of 100 nonschizophrenic males, the schizophrenogenic mothers turned out to be both excessively devoted *and* coolly detached (Mark, 1953). The findings regarding schizophrenogenic mothers, in short, have been extremely vague and contradictory.

Some of the more revealing findings regarding the early environment of the schizophrenic come from considering *interparental* behavior patterns rather than merely focusing on the mother. Garmezy, Clarke, and Stockner (1961) gave a child rearing attitude scale to process and reactive schizophrenics as well as to a normal group, and asked them to answer the items on the scale in the way they felt their mothers *and* fathers might have answered when they (the subjects) were growing up. The authors found that process schizophrenics assigned more deviant attitudes to both parents than did reactive schizophrenics and normals, and furthermore noted that a maternal dominance pattern reported among process patients was reversed in reactives. Among reactive patients, paternal dominance was the rule.

These findings were corroborated and expanded in a laboratory study by Farina (1960). In order to investigate interactional patterns in schizophrenic families *in vivo*, Farina brought the parents of schizophrenics directly into the laboratory and asked them to solve a series of problems. The problems consisted of twelve hypothetical situations depicting some type of conflict between parent and son. Some examples are:

> A gang of boys calls to your eight-year-old son to come out and play. You don't think it's good for your son to play with these boys, but now he starts to leave the house to go with them.

> Your seventeen-year-old son has a chance to take a job which you are sure would be good for him. He knows you would like him to take it but he doesn't want it. Instead, he wants to take a job which you think would not be good for him.

The parents were first asked to come up with independent solutions and then required to meet as a pair and decide upon a cooperative answer. Farina analyzed their interactional behavior with particular emphasis on patterns of dominance and conflict.

The indices used to chart dominance and conflict were extracted from the pair's interactional behavior during the conjoint session. Some of the dominance measures employed include who speaks first, who speaks the most, and the number of times one parent yields to the other's solution. Typical indices of conflict included the number of interruptions, the number of disagreements, and the frequency of simultaneous speech.

The findings are complex because of the many indices used for each category of interaction and because of the number of group comparisons carried out. Nevertheless, they summed up in Figure 7, shown below. As Figure 7 indicates, the interpersonal dominance patterns among parents of process and reactive schizophrenics are the inverse of one another. In addition, it appears that children who become process schizophrenics are probably exposed to a highly conflictual home environment. The Farina study demonstrates the importance of considering interparental as well as parent-child relationships in schizophrenic families, and once again points up the value of distinguishing between process and reactive schizophrenia in research dealing with origins.

**The regression hypothesis.** This approach to understanding the origins of schizophrenia derives from psychoanalytic personality theory. In this formulation, the schizophrenic's unusual behavior is viewed as a reflection of a basic personality fault whose presence predisposes the patient to return to childlike levels of functioning under stressful circumstances.

According to psychoanalytic theory, the schizophrenic's tendency to revert to infantile behavior, to regress, results from negative emotional experiences that occur in his first few years. During this period, when children have to cope with one maturational challenge after another, the stance

| | DOMINANCE | | CONFLICT |
|---|---|---|---|
| | Mother | Father | |
| Reactive Schizophrenics | Weak and submissive | Markedly dominant | Moderate |
| Process Schizophrenics | Markedly dominant | Moderately submissive | Great |
| Normals | Shared pattern of authority | | Very little |

FIGURE 7.    Dominance and conflict patterns in parents of schizophrenics. After Farina (1960).

adopted by parents tends to be of utmost importance. Parents who encourage the child's attempts at mastery and intercede only when truly necessary are thought to contribute to optimal psychological development. The parents of schizophrenics, particularly the mothers, are presumed to deviate significantly from this norm. Psychoanalytic theory proposes that the mothers of schizophrenics are either emotionally detached from their children *or* overprotective toward them.

When the mother-child relationship is characterized by emotional detachment, the child experiences a marked coolness in his interactions with the one person who could best provide him with nurturance and warmth. Though the mother ministers to the child's basic needs, she perceives him as a psychological liability and virtually ignores him. The child, as a result, comes to perceive interpersonal relationships as ungratifying and threatening; he ultimately withdraws from others and becomes socially isolated.

The overprotected child, in contrast, is provided with too much attention. He is virtually smothered with solicitous care to the extent that he is unable to strike out on his own and develop a separate identity. In such instances, referred to as *symbiosis* (*sym* = together; *bios* = life), the mother and child become an inseparable unit. Whether the child is overprotected or deprived of love, the result in both cases is obstructed psychological growth.

In Chapter 1, we demonstrated how both the deprived and overindulged child have a tendency to become psychologically bogged down, or *fixated*, in one of the early stages of growth. Both the detached and the symbiotic child represent extreme instances of fixation. Their difficulty is accentuated by the fact that in their case, fixation has occurred in the earliest, or oral, stage of development. Since optimal negotiation of succeeding stages depends to some extent on early successes and failures, these children are grossly disadvantaged. Although they grow up physically and intellectually, they are conspicuously lacking in the social skills needed to cope with the challenges of everyday life. They are characterized by an infantile personality structure and are inclined to deal with the world in immature ways; under stress such persons are apt to slip into behavior patterns reflecting an earlier level of development. The tendency to respond in this way, to regress, forms the basis for schizophrenic behavior.

The concept of regression, the recurrent appearance of responses that are maturationally inappropriate, is closely tied to the concept of fixation, for it is to an earlier level of fixation that the individual regresses. However, not all regressive behavior is psychotic or even pathological. For example, the child who experiences severe frustration during toilet training may revert to baby talk or suck his thumb; the adult who gets angry and frustrated may occasionally have a temper tantrum. But behavior of this sort is infrequent in normals, while it is common in schizophrenics. Furthermore, regression in the schizophrenic is deeper—his behavior reverts back to the earliest stage of development. The patient may then have to be fed, led to the bathroom, and directed in the simplest tasks.

The conditions under which regression occurs in adults usually result from intensive or prolonged stress. Stress of this sort may emanate from internal sources, such as overwhelming id impulses, or from external threats in the environment. Whether the patient is experiencing a strong urge to harm someone, a homosexual impulse, loss of a job, or failure in school, he finds himself strained beyond his capacity. Experiences of this sort, while they often cause serious distress in normals, drive the potential schizophrenic to a point where he can no longer function adequately. It is under such circumstances that psychotic behavior is likely to emerge.

Regression theory can be applied to a variety of psychotic behaviors, many of which have to do with sexual and aggressive behavior. Mature behavior in these areas typically connotes an ability to moderate, and, if necessary, to delay one's responses. Because of obstructions in the normal course of development, the schizophrenic lacks the inner controls that enable him to do this. Whatever controls do exist are too weak to counterbalance momentary urges. If he feels angry, he is likely to strike out at something or someone with very little provocation; if he becomes sexually aroused, he may publicly masturbate. What makes this psychotic is not the behavior, per se, but its presence in a biologically mature individual; the same behavior in an infant would not be particularly alarming.

The behavioral regression described above is paralleled by regression in the patient's thought processes. Recalling the progression of id to ego functioning in normal maturation, it is not surprising to find the schizophrenic's mental processes largely guided by the id. This essentially means that the irrational and wish fulfilling nature of infantile thought now begins to dominate the adult's thinking processes. Omnipotent childhood fantasies dealing with godly powers and magical skills, fantasies sacrificed earlier for the sake of realistic functioning, once again begin to predominate. If the schizophrenic desires to be talented and world-renowned, he has only to wish it; if he wishes to fly he can create a world of fantasy in which men have wings. Nothing is beyond his power.

In much the same way that a bored school child spends his time daydreaming about colorful places and exciting adventures, so the schizophrenic retreats into a make-believe world. But unlike the child who has learned in the course of normal development to distinguish between fact and fantasy, the schizophrenic cannot. The distinction between fantasy and reality has become blurred and the more he escapes to the private world he has created, the more difficult it is for him to function in the real world.

The regression theory of schizophrenia, in sum, is able to explain a great deal of psychotic symptomatology. The behavior of the hospitalized schizophrenic who eats with his fingers and soils his clothes is explained as a primitive throwback to the earliest stage of development. The patient's auditory and visual hallucinations as well as his tendency toward social isolation, are seen as a direct consequence of his immersion in fantasy. The schizophrenic, in short, has become less responsive to external stimuli and more attentive to internally produced wishes and impulses. To the extent that one accepts the psychoanalytic point of view, the regression hypothesis provides a powerful means of explaining a wide range of schizophrenic behavior.

**The double-bind hypothesis.** Human interaction is often intricate and difficult to understand. However, one way of understanding social relationships is through an analysis of human communications. The double-bind theory is an approach that describes deviant behavior in terms of deviant communication patterns, the origins of which are thought to lie in childhood.

In contrast to regression theory which sees the schizophrenic's bizarre speech patterns as an expression of primitive fantasies, the double-bind hypothesis portrays the schizophrenic's use of language as the means by which he structures his relationships. His confusing utterances are not seen as infantile or random but as relatively purposeful and deliberate; in their very ambiguity, they keep the schizophrenic interpersonally uncommitted and safe from dangerous involvement. The growth of deviant communication patterns is synonymous with the growth of psychopathology.

According to current thought on the nature of communications, all human exchanges contain important messages. This is true even for those exchanges devoid of verbal interaction; silences, furrowed brows, and bored looks convey information as effectively as words. The term "communication," therefore, includes many different ways of sending and receiving information.

Among the different types of messages that people transmit are communications that tell us something about other communications. These are referred to as *metacommunications* (*meta* = beyond) and encompass vocal intonations, body gestures, smiles, and frowns. The comments, "She's pretty!" and "She's pretty?" have two very different meanings. A smile that accompanies a negative remark indicates that what has been said should not be taken very seriously. No matter what form metacommunications take, they either affirm, negate, or qualify one's verbal statements.[1]

In most social interchanges, communications and metacommunications are congruent. Friendly smiles usually go hand in hand with friendly words, and scowls accompany scoldings. But often they are not. When this occurs,

---

[1]Although metacommunications are, for the most part, nonverbal, they can also be verbal; a common example is the use of the comment "I was only kidding" to negate the statement preceding it.

it is imperative to know how to discriminate between different types of messages. The person who has difficulty in determining whether other people mean what they say or are joking will find interpersonal relationships hazardous. The schizophrenic is such a person.

The type of situation in childhood that is responsible for difficulty of this sort is a complex interaction involving a manipulator and his victim. The victim is exposed to messages that tell him how to behave but at the same time contain information that is basically contradictory. All of his choices therefore are doomed to failure. The victim's dilemma, the *double bind*, is highlighted in the story of the mother who asks her son whether he wants lamb chops or pot roast for supper. When he responds lamb chops, she asks in a pained tone, "Don't you like my pot roast?"

The proponents of the double-bind hypothesis draws a parallel between the predicament of the double-bind victim and the dilemma faced by a pupil of Zen Buddhism.

> The Zen Master attempts to bring about enlightenment in his pupil in various ways. One of the things he does is to hold a stick over the pupil's head and say fiercely, "If you say this stick is real, I will strike you with it. If you say this stick is not real, I will strike you with it. If you don't say anything, I will strike you with it." We feel that the schizophrenic finds himself continually in the same situation as the pupil, but he achieves something like disorientation rather than enlightenment. (Bateson *et al.*, 1956, p. 154)

According to this view, the consequences of such a predicament can be devastating, especially when the victim is a young child and the process is repeated over and over.

The basic ingredients for a double bind most often are a young child and an adult family member, usually the mother, upon whom the child is physically and emotionally dependent. Although the mother would like to see herself as loving and devoted, she is fearful of closeness; intimacy for her leads to heightened anxiety and even panic. This is a woman who harbors a great deal of ambivalence about her maternal competence.

The mother's ambivalence is reflected in the conflicting messages she transmits to the child. On one hand, she sends overt messages of affection (for example, "Mother loves you"), messages that are essentially transmitted through verbal channels. These, however, are accompanied by metacommunications that signify just the opposite. Whenever the child comes too close, the mother acts coolly, speaks sharply, and tends to withdraw. The child obviously must make critical discriminations if he is to respond appropriately.

Let us trace the consequences of the child's behavior, first when his discriminations are accurate, and then when they are inaccurate. The child who accurately distinguishes between the two orders of messages that the mother transmits has to face the fact that (1) she does not love him, and (2) she is trying to deceive him. Assuming this to be the case, he most likely will cease making affectionate overtures and eventually withdraw. This poses a threat to the mother's perception of herself as a loving mother and she punishes him. Punishment may involve guilt induction ("Don't you love me any more?") or depreciation of the child's worth ("You don't deserve the attention I give you"). It need not be, and usually is not, physical punishment. Whatever form it takes, it directly follows from the child's *accurate discrimination* of the mother's conflicting messages.

The child who falsely discriminates what the mother is transmitting, closes his eyes, so to speak, to her metacommunicative signals. He accepts her counterfeit love and approaches her with overtures of affection. But as the distance between them lessens, the mother gets very anxious and puts the child off. And if he persists, *she* withdraws. The child, as a consequence, is punished by being cut off from close and intimate association with the one figure upon whom he must depend. Punishment in this instance results from *inaccurate discrimination* of communicative and metacommunicative signals. Here we see the double bind—a "heads I win, tails you lose" predicament in which the child is punished for both discriminating falsely *and* for discriminating accurately.

Is there any way to break out of this "no win" predicament? One thing the child might do is call attention to his difficult position, complaining to the mother about her contradictory messages. But this is a difficult thing for a young child to do. Even if he were able to do it with some degree of finesse, the mother might still take this as an accusation that she is unloving and punish him even more; at the very least, she would insist that his perception is distorted. As an alternative, the child could conceivably fall back on the father, hoping to enlist his aid in escaping the mother's subtle manipulations. But the authors of the double bind indicate that fathers of schizophrenics tend to be rather weak figures who are unable to provide the patient with meaningful help.

As a result of the double bind, the child may grow up learning that it is best to keep his relationships with others vague and ambiguous. To accomplish this, he often denies transmitting or receiving interpersonal information. The schizophrenic denies transmitting information via persistent claims that someone else, not he, is speaking. We thus encounter patients who claim they are great oracles such as Moses or Jesus Christ. He denies *receiving* messages by claiming that a machine interferes with what other people say or that a device implanted in his brain acts to filter out their irrelevant remarks. Since the transmission and reception of messages is an essential feature of all human interaction, the result is alienation from others and increased social withdrawal.

The double-bind hypothesis, in sum, attempts to explain many of the major symptoms of schizophrenia by means of communication theory. According to this formulation, schizophrenic behaviors are deviant communications that help the patient avert the interpersonal rejection he has learned to anticipate throughout his life. The origins of these avoidance patterns are traced to subtle but devastating mother-child interactions that are repeated throughout the patient's early years. Labeled the double bind, they predispose the patient to behave in psychotic ways in adulthood.

The approaches to the study of schizophrenia just described represent three different attempts to resolve etiological issues. The process-reactive formulation, distinguishing between patients for whom the onset and outcome of the disorder differ, is basically descriptive in character. Nevertheless, it yields tight, quantifiable hypotheses regarding the nature of the schizophrenic's early family life. These, as we saw, led to some interesting findings concerning the relation of one parent to the other in schizophrenic families. The double-bind and regression hypotheses, in comparison, are large scale formulations and tend to be more explanatory in nature. Taking rather divergent paths, they attempt to explain a wide variety of pathological behavior by theoretically describing the implications of a developmental process gone awry. Like process-reactive research, they represent approaches to the complex topic of origins.

### SYMPTOM PROCESSES IN SCHIZOPHRENIA

In the preceding section we presented several formulations that are concerned with the causes of schizophrenia. The disturbance can also be approached from a different viewpoint. If a person is psychotic, one may inquire into the processes that underlie his strange behavior rather than its origins. Most formulations of this sort tend to focus on current distortions in the patient's perception and cognition. In this section, we will examine three lines of inquiry into schizophrenic thought processes: the concepts of overinclusive thinking, the interference hypothesis, and cognitive closure.

**Overinclusive thinking.** From Bleuler's time to the present, the schizophrenic's tendency towards fragmented speech and bizarre conceptual thinking has been regarded as one of the primary features of the disorder. Much of the psychological research in schizophrenia, accordingly, has revolved about irregularities in the patient's use of language and his ability to form concepts. One segment of the literature that deals directly with the processes underlying these irregularities is subsumed under the broad title of overinclusive thinking.

Overinclusion refers to the tendency of seemingly irrelevant responses to interfere with normal thought and speech patterns. It is used to describe the persistent intrusion of inconsequential elements in an ongoing task, and is not an uncommon phenomenon. Most of us have at one time or another tried to complete a task while having to contend with bothersome and disruptive thoughts. For example, a student may struggle with a home-work assignment on Thursday evening only to have thoughts of the up-coming weekend interfere with his ability to concentrate. In most cases of this sort, overinclusion is fleeting; it does not lead to endless interrup-tions. In schizophrenia, overinclusion is allegedly more pervasive, con-stantly interfering with the patient's ability to function.

A number of studies have been designed to empirically test the hy-pothesis that schizophrenics do, in fact, overinclude more than normals. In one such study, Epstein (1953) compared the performance of normals and schizophrenics on an overinclusion test, a task he personally con-structed to measure overinclusive tendencies. The test was comprised of fifty items, each of which contained a key stimulus word and several responses needed to describe it. Included among the correct responses were a number of irrelevant, or incorrect, responses. The following is a sample test item with **MAN** as the stimulus.

**MAN:**    arms    shoes    hat    toes    head    none

The object of the task was to underline all the responses that described necessary parts of the key word. If the subject felt that none of the words were appropriate, he simply underlined "none."

In the sample provided the correct responses are, of course, *arms, toes* and *head*. All other responses are irrelevant and, if underlined, constitute instances of overinclusion. A person's overinclusion score is the total number of incorrect responses. Other examples of test items are:

**HOUSE:**    walls    curtains    telephone    bricks    roof    none
**CAT:**    beard    whiskers    milk    kitten    mouse    none

The test was administered to schizophrenic and normal subjects and the average number of incorrect responses computed for each group. The results were clearcut. Normals averaged 12.5 errors on the test while schizophrenics averaged 20.9. The difference between the two groups was highly significant statistically, confirming the hypothesis that schizophrenics do overinclude more than normals.

The question nevertheless remains as to the precise character of over-inclusive responses. Epstein, in his article, suggests that such errors are not simply made on a random basis. Analyzing the responses of his sample, he noted that schizophrenics seem to make either concrete errors, for example choosing *wood* as necessary to **BOX**, or they "choose response words which are . . . only superficially and associationistically related to the key word. . . ." (1953, p. 386). There thus appears to be some order within the seemingly chaotic response pattern of schizophrenic patients.

Following up this observation, Chapman and Taylor (1957) set out to construct a task that would directly assess a subject's tendency to make associative vs. nonassociative errors. Their search led them to a standard sorting task used in concept formation experiments. In experiments of this sort, the subject is required to discriminate between correct and incorrect instances of a concept by sorting stimuli in appropriate categories. If, for example, he is given three cards with the words *oak, fish,* and *hammer* on them and asked to sort them into two piles—**TREES** and **NOT-TREES**—he must obviously place *oak* in the **TREE** pile and the other two in the **NOT-TREE** pile. If either *fish* or *hammer* (or both) are incorrectly assigned, they are considered overinclusions. We should note that, if a tendency towards overinclusion exists, there is no reason to expect one incorrect response to occur more often than the other.

Chapman and Taylor adapted this task for their purposes by making one significant change. One of the two *incorrect* responses was made more associatively similar to the concept than the other. If, in the previous example, the three stimuli were comprised of *oak, hammer,* and *leaf, leaf* would be an example of an *incorrect but similar* response because it is a fairly common association to tree. It nevertheless is incorrect as an example of a tree. Hammer, on the other hand, is an example of an *incorrect-dissimilar* response. If a subject's overinclusions are based on associative errors, he should missort incorrect-similar items more often than incorrect-dissimilar ones. Figure 8 demonstrates a correct sort as well as two types of overinclusive, or incorrect, sorts.

Some examples of test items devised by Chapman and Taylor are:

| | | | |
|---|---|---|---|
| beer | milk | spider | (concept: ALCOHOLIC BEVERAGES) |
| tiger | cow | boat | (concept: WILD ANIMALS) |

In the first case, both *milk* and *spider* are *incorrect* responses; *milk,* however, bears more associative similarity to the concept because it is a beverage. In the second example *cow* would be an incorrect but similar response; the concept is WILD ANIMAL, not animal.

Using this as a guideline, a series of additional test items were constructed, each containing a correct response, an incorrect-dissimilar response, and an incorrect-similar response. The test was administered to a group of normals and two groups of schizophrenics, one moderately and the other severely disturbed. The results for all three groups are presented in Table 3. Scores in the table represent the average number of incorrect placements for each group. It is apparent that while normals make very few overinclusions of any sort, schizophrenics, irrespective of whether they

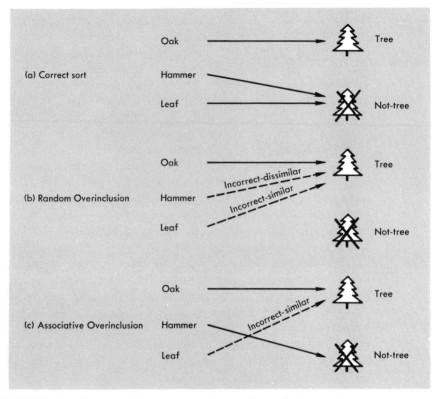

FIGURE 8.    Correct and incorrect (random and associative) sorts.

are moderately or severely disturbed, make many more overinclusions of the "similar" type; they make the type of errors depicted in Fig 8c. One may conclude on the basis of this study that overinclusion in schizophrenia is not a random process but rather is based on superficial and tangential associations.

The concept of overinclusion, in sum, is one of a number of theoretical devices used to explain some of the unusual behavior seen in schizophrenia. Most of the research on the topic, only a portion of which was described, indicates that schizophrenics do overinclude more than normals. The character of overinclusive errors, moreover, seems to be dictated by associative rather than random considerations. Further investigation into the schizophrenic's associative processes is depicted in a formulation called the interference hypothesis.

**The interference hypothesis.**    According to many clinicians and researchers, the loose associations that characterize schizophrenic thought represent the disorder's fundamental defect. The interference hypothesis

## Table 3

*Mean Number of Errors on Sorting Task*

| GROUP | OVERINCLUSIONS | |
|---|---|---|
| | *Similar* | *Dissimilar* |
| Normals | .54 | .33 |
| Schizophrenic (moderate) | 7.33 | .29 |
| Schizophrenic (severe) | 8.20 | 1.33 |

Adapted from Chapman and Taylor, (1957, p. 121).

is an attempt to explain the various symptoms of schizophrenia through analyzing the way in which loose associations disrupt, or interfere, with the patient's mental processes. Within this formulation, major importance is attributed to the concepts of an "associative hierarchy" and "arousal."

An *associative hierarchy* is the tendency of a stimulus word to evoke a number of different responses, some of which are more probable than others. Thus, the dominant response to BOY is *girl* rather than *young* or *man*. The associative hierarchy for BOY is likely to contain in order of decreasing associative strength, such responses as *girl, man, person, young, son*, and so on. At the very bottom of the hierarchy one might even find the word *toy*, a rare response whose association to BOY is based more on similarity in sound than anything else. An associative hierarchy thus is essentially a pattern of dominant (strong) and subsidiary (weak) responses, each of which differs in strength according to past learning.

Since most stimuli are capable of evoking many different responses, the various responses may compete and potentially interfere with each other. This is most likely to occur when the associations are close in strength. In the foregoing example, *girl* and *man* will tend to be highly competitive since they both constitute strong associations to BOY. *Girl* and *toy*, in contrast, are least likely to compete since their strengths differ so markedly. The greater the difference in strength between a dominant and competing response, the less likely it is that the two will interfere with one another. In schizophrenia, it is hypothesized that normal hierarchical relationships such as these break down, leading to the frequent interference of dominant by weak responses. This, in turn, disrupts speech and other cognitive functions.

Before examining the precise conditions under which this disruption occurs, it is necessary to consider the concept of *arousal*. Arousal refers to a diffuse state of mental and physical activation that can be measured through changes in respiration rate, heart rate, and the galvanic skin response. Heightened arousal is often associated with states of panic and anger, and in many cases of psychopathology, is synonymous with anxiety.

Under normal circumstances arousal facilitates performance on learning tasks by increasing the strength of dominant responses. As arousal increases, so does task performance. But after a point (the "arousal ceiling"), increased arousal only produces disorganization. Research has shown, for example, that students who are moderately anxious or "up" for an exam perform better than students who remain relatively unaroused. Highly anxious students, however, are more likely to do poorly than their moderately anxious classmates.

A similar reaction is often seen in the case of the beginning driver. Prior to taking his driving test, the novice may perform quite competently behind the wheel, even though he is a little nervous. But during the test this suddenly changes as he finds himself getting increasingly anxious. He turns the wheel to the right when told to turn left, steps on the gas when told to stop, and makes other devastating errors. Incorrect responses that were low on his response hierarchy have, under increased arousal, become dominant. The interference hypothesis suggests that a similar form of disorganization occurs in schizophrenia.

The process through which this disorganization occurs is described by Broen and Storms (1966), two psychologists who are among the most articulate spokesmen for the interference hypothesis. They believe schizophrenia involves a breakdown in associative hierarchies that in turn leads to the emergence of previously weak responses. By assuming that response ceilings for arousal are abnormally low in schizophrenics, they attempt to describe the process by which schizophrenic behavior becomes disorganized and unpredictable.

The analysis that Broen and Storms present can be graphically portrayed by imagining a set of balloons suspended in a tank of liquid (see Figure 9). The balloons depict various associations in a response hierarchy; the dominant response is labeled $R_1$, with $R_2$ and $R_3$ denoting weaker, competing responses. The principal difference between the normal and schizophrenic conditions is that the ceiling levels for arousal differ.

Comparing Figures 9a and 9b, one can see that the dominance patterns in both cases are very similar. The relative position of $R_1$ with regard to its two competing responses is, in both cases, practically identical. But let us see what happens when the level of arousal increases (represented by the balloons rising in the liquid). In the case of normals, increased arousal results in an increase in the strength of both dominant *and* competing responses. The relative difference between $R_1$, $R_2$, and $R_3$ therefore remains the same under low and high arousal.

The same increase in arousal leads to vastly different consequences in

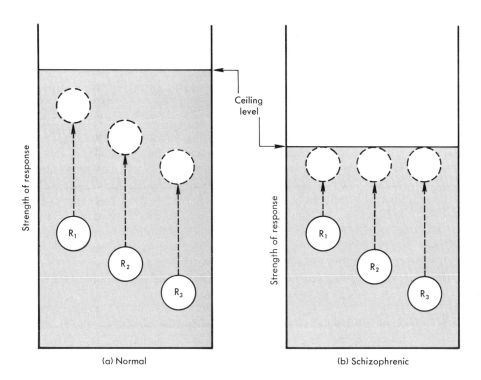

(a) Normal                                           (b) Schizophrenic

FIGURE 9.    Associative hierarchies for normals and schizophrenics.

schizophrenics, as shown in Figure 9*b*. Since there is a lower ceiling, only a small amount of arousal is needed to bring the dominant response to ceiling. All that increased arousal manages to do in the case of the schizophrenic is bring competing responses up to the same level. Dominant and competing responses have now become equal in strength, and the hierarchical dominance pattern that earlier was in evidence no longer exists.

This indicates that remote associations to stimulus words or questions are as likely to be evoked as common associations in schizophrenics, illustrating why the schizophrenic patient is likely to give unusual responses to such simple questions as, "Who is the president of the United States?" To this, he is as likely to respond "George Washington" or "The White House" as he is to give the correct answer.

The interference hypothesis, like the regression hypothesis, can be used to explain a wide range of phenomena. It is obviously most applicable in situations where associative processes are involved. We have already seen how it may be invoked to explain the schizophrenic's deviant use of language. It also can be used to explain the onset of delusions.

In the initial stages of delusion formation, the potential schizophrenic is faced with the problem of reconciling a number of confusing and upsetting events. Loss of a job, failure in school, and serious difficulties with other people are not only perplexing but lead to heightened arousal. Attempts to reconcile such problems may result in both relevant and irrelevant associations; these must then be separated so that realistic answers can be arrived at. Sometimes this process goes awry, particularly if the arousal ceiling of the individual is low.

A schizophrenic patient, recounting the incidents leading to his hospitalization, told of an event that signalled the beginning of his delusions. The patient woke one morning with a hangover and went down to the kitchen where his wife was preparing breakfast. As he sipped his orange juice, he thought it tasted funny and started to feel angry. He started wondering why the juice tasted so vile and several associations came to him:

1. the juice was squeezed from a bad batch of oranges;
2. his hangover had deadened his taste buds;
3. his wife was trying to poison him.

Remembering that his wife had looked at him strangely in recent days, he chose the third alternative and concluded that she was trying to get rid of him. This ultimately developed into an intricate delusion involving a secret murder-for-hire organization. The patient, convinced that his wife had secured the services of a killer, responded by fleeing to another city and going into hiding.

Single incidents such as this do not fully explain the development of delusional beliefs. In this particular case, it is worthwhile noting that the patient was always a suspicious, untrusting individual, and that his marital relationship was far from satisfactory. A more potent criticism of the interference hypothesis is that it leaves the basis for the "low arousal ceiling" unexplained. What exactly is its nature? Is there any way of independently assessing whether any given person, schizophrenic or otherwise, has a low ceiling? Until the precise character of this defect is spelled out more fully, the interference hypothesis falls short of its potential.

**Cognitive closure.** The concept of closure had its beginning in early perceptual experiments dealing with the tendency of people to improve irregular or incomplete figures. Given a picture of an unclosed circle or a line with a small segment missing, subjects would fill in, or close, the gap. In the past few years, this finding has been extended to formulations of cognitive functioning. Accordingly, it has been proposed that certain persons, confronted with incomplete or vague situations, are apt to seek quick, and sometimes premature solutions. This hypothesis has recently been tested in a series of studies dealing with the process underlying delusion formation.

Within this line of research, central importance is given to the fact that life is often filled with ambiguous circumstances and that ambiguity often produces anxiety. A close examination of any person's daily affairs indicates that many of his experiences are characterized by ambiguity and apprehension. Joining a new group, going on a blind date, and preparing for a difficult exam, are all examples of ambiguous situations associated with varying degrees of anxiety. It is not unusual, therefore, to find that people try to reduce ambiguity whenever confronted with it.

One common technique for reducing ambiguity involves seeking out more relevant information; this is what most people do if given the opportunity. Another technique involves jumping to conclusions on the basis of the information at hand. This is the course adopted when a fast decision is needed and there is no time to gather additional data. In both cases, the desired end result is *closure*—the resolution of an open-ended, or ambiguous, situation.

It should be recognized that while the second approach can resolve ambiguity as well as the first, it involves greater risk. In situations involving premature judgments, errors are more likely to occur. And errors, particularly those regarding the motives of others, can form the basis for false and sometimes preposterous beliefs. When such beliefs deviate sharply from the rest of society's beliefs and also interfere with one's daily functioning, they fall into the category of delusions. A delusion can be seen as the end result of a process in which a decision is prematurely reached under highly ambiguous circumstances. Once arrived at, such decisions are highly resistant to change since they help the patient make sense of an otherwise confusing and anxiety provoking situation; that is, they provide closure.

An example of this process was seen earlier in the case of the patient who tried to figure out why his orange juice tasted so strange. Confronted with ambiguous circumstances (strange-tasting orange juice and his wife's "funny glances"), he prematurely concluded that his wife was trying to kill him. While such a conclusion was threatening in itself, it at least allowed him to achieve closure and take some sort of action.

If the foregoing process represents what occurs in delusion formation, we should expect delusional schizophrenics to display a greater tendency towards closure than nondelusional schizophrenics. To test this hypothesis, McReynolds *et al.* (1964) examined the behavior of delusional and nondelusional patients on a perceptual ambiguity task called the McGill Closure Test (Mooney and Ferguson, 1951). This test consists of a number of incomplete pictures of common objects or simple scenes. Each item is fragmented so that the identity of the object or the nature of the scene is ambiguous. Several of the test items are presented in Figure 10. A person's score on the test (the number of identifications he attempts) is designed to reflect his discomfort with ambiguity.

FIGURE 10. Items from the Mc-Gill Closure Test: *left*, a cowboy on a bucking bronco; *below*, a man and woman dancing. From Mooney and Ferguson (1951).

McReynolds exposed delusional and nondelusional subjects to each test item for 25 seconds and tallied the number of identifications they attempted. The average score for each subject was computed and taken as a measure of his tendency to seek closure. As expected, patients in the delusional group attempted significantly more identifications than those in the nondelusional group. The hypothesis of a positive relation between the presence of delusions and closure tendencies therefore was supported.

Not all studies in this area have yielded such clear-cut results. In one study (Cashdan, 1966), interest centered on the *amount* of information that subjects would sample before they made an attempt to resolve an ambiguous situation. McReynolds' task measured only whether subjects were willing to take a guess, not how much information they used. A different type of task therefore was needed to allow the information yield of each stimulus to be varied.

The task settled upon required subjects to judge the identity of common objects presented in distorted (ambiguous) fashion (Draguns, 1963). Each trial consisted of a series of twelve differentially blurred photographs of the same object. The first photo in the series was essentially unrecognizable while the last was perfectly in focus. As the subject is exposed to each photograph in sequence, he is provided with more information about the object's identity. His job is to notify the examiner whenever he feels he has an idea of what the object is. The task is repeated with many common objects (dog, house, tree, etc.), with the subject's "recognition level" computed as his average score for the different objects.

The task was administered to three groups of subjects: schizophrenics with marked delusions, schizophrenics who showed little evidence of delusions, and normals. The scores could range from one to twelve, with lower scores reflecting a tendency towards early closure. The study's major hypothesis was that the maximally delusional patients would make more premature guesses and score lower than minimally delusional subjects.

The results of the study, however, did not support the hypothesis. The two schizophrenic groups performed in approximately the same fashion, averaging a score of six on the task. Interestingly enough, very few patients guessed at the sixth slide; they guessed at either slide two or slide ten. The average score of six disguised the fact that the schizophrenic distribution for both groups was bimodal. Irrespective of whether they were delusional or not, approximately half the patients jumped to premature conclusions while the other half waited until almost the very end. Since most normal subjects made correct judgments at approximately the eighth slide, it seems that the late responding group of schizophrenics may have been a little too cautious; they could have made their decision earlier and still have been correct.

While findings of this sort require replication, they suggest that the relation between closure tendencies and delusion formation may be more complex than earlier believed. Information processing in schizophrenics may include tendencies toward delayed judgment *as well as* tendencies towards premature closure. Only future research will help reconcile the apparent discrepancies in the studies discussed.

Each of the formulations presented in this section, like those in the preceding section, differ according to the breadth of phenomena they try to explain. The overinclusion and closure hypotheses tend to be somewhat limited in application while the interference hypothesis is more ambitious in scope. Each nevertheless represents a unique approach to the mechanisms underlying schizophrenic symptoms. Together with the formulations centering on origins, they contribute to a better understanding of what is probably the most complex subject in the entire realm of abnormal psychology.

The major alternatives to the formulations described above are organic in nature. In Chapter 1 we stated that the organic model does not enjoy widespread recognition among modern clinicians. Nevertheless, it has remained fairly visible in the area of psychosis. Accordingly, a fair amount of theorizing and research in the area of schizophrenia tends to emphasize genetic and biochemical variables. In the following section, we present some of the formulations associated with the biological perspective, concluding the chapter with an examination of the sociological perspective.

## The Biological Perspective

The general belief that the origins of schizophrenia lay in some form of brain damage gained popularity in the 1800s and was reflected in Kraepelin's conceptualization of *dementia praecox*. Today, as a result of advances in statistics and microbiology, this notion exists in a more sophisticated form and is represented in the research on genetic and biochemical correlates of schizophrenic behavior.

### GENETIC CORRELATES

The research linking schizophrenia to hereditary factors had its beginnings in reports that the disorder runs in families. This clinical observation was corroborated by statistical data indicating that the closer a blood relative is to a schizophrenic, the more likely it is that he too will develop the disorder. Approximately 15 percent of a schizophrenic's siblings also are schizophrenic, while the figure is closer to 4 or 5 percent among nieces and nephews. The relationship between heredity and schizophrenia gains further support by the finding that 16 percent of children with one schizophrenic parent develop the disorder while the corresponding figure for children with two schizophrenic parents is 68 percent (Kallman, 1946). Figure 11 summarizes some of these statistical findings.

Despite such impressive figures, one cannot, on the basis of this evidence

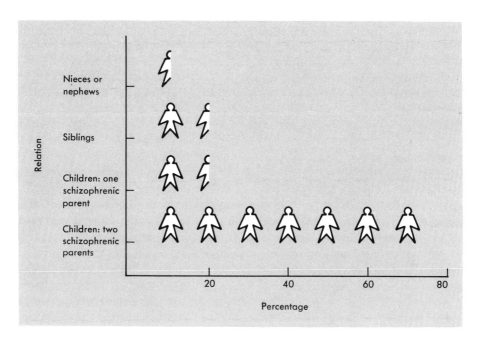

FIGURE 11.   Incidence of schizophrenia among relatives of schizophrenic patients. After Kallman (1946).

alone, confidently conclude that schizophrenia is a genetic disorder. Constant exposure to a psychotic parent can by itself account for such high figures. Being raised by two schizophrenic parents, moreover, is probably more than twice as stressful as being raised by one. With one, the child at least can seek out the other for temporary refuge. Environmental factors, in short, cannot be ruled out. For this reason much of the genetic research has centered on the study of schizophrenic twins.

Twin studies attempt to assess the relative contribution of genetic and environmental factors through a comparison of schizophrenia in identical and fraternal twins. The reasoning behind this approach is fairly straightforward. Identical, or *monozygotic* (single cell) twins share a common hereditary makeup; their genetic patterns are exactly alike. Fraternal, or *dizygotic* (two cell) twins have similar but not identical patterns; their genetic makeup parallels that of regular siblings. It follows that if schizophrenia is inherited, it should turn up more often in both members of a monozygotic twin pair than in the members of dizygotic pairs.

The measure used to test this hypothesis is called the *concordance rate* and refers to the percentage of cases in which both members of a twin pair have schizophrenia. Table 4 summarizes a number of major studies in which monozygotic (MZ) and dizygotic (DZ) twins were compared. As can be seen, the differences between concordance rates for monozy-

## Table 4

Concordance Rates in MZ and DZ Co-Twins of Schizophrenics

| INVESTIGATOR | CONCORDANCE RATE (%) | |
|---|---|---|
|  | MZ | DZ |
| Rosanoff, 1934 | 68 | 15 |
| Essen-Moller, 1941 | 71 | 17 |
| Slater, 1953 | 76 | 14 |
| Kallman, 1953 | 86 | 15 |

gotic and dizygotic twins are not only quite large but are consistent from study to study. Furthermore, the rates for dizygotic twins are close to the 15 percent rate quoted earlier for nontwin siblings. The case for a genetic component in schizophrenia, therefore, derives support from studies employing twin comparisons.

Nevertheless, evidence even as strong as this has been challenged on psychological grounds. Most identical twins are exposed to highly similar environments (they are dressed alike, responded to similarly, and so on) so there is a much greater likelihood of their turning out to be like one another than with fraternal twins. This in itself could account for the exaggerated concordance rates.

Twin studies, in addition, have received their share of criticism on methodological grounds. Many early studies, for one, contained errors in judgments of zygosity. It is not enough to infer the presence of monozygosity merely on the basis of body and facial characteristics; many fraternal twins are look alikes and serum tests are required for an accurate assessment. Second, many of the original twin studies did not contain double-blind precautions. That is to say, the investigator who judged zygosity also judged the presence or absence of schizophrenia. In double-blind studies, such judgments are made independently. For example, in drug research the person who administers the drug is not the same person who judges whether or not the patient improves. This scientific precaution guards against the experimenter unwittingly biasing his hypothesis in a favorable direction.

Despite these criticisms, the weight of the evidence still seems to support the hypothesis of hereditary involvement. But most investigators believe that even if a genetic factor is involved, it simply predisposes one towards the disorder's development. Kallman, a renowned psychiatric geneticist, believes that one can only predict hereditary *tendencies* and that environmental factors must always be considered (1953). Paul Meehl's notion of schizotaxia-schizotypia (1962), discussed in Chapter 1, exemplifies this position. At best, hereditary factors interact with psychological factors to produce schizophrenic syndromes.

BIOCHEMICAL CORRELATES

Assuming that biological factors are involved in schizophrenia, one should be able to detect this in the schizophrenic's body chemistry. Many people claim to have done just this. Research reports that cite deviations in the schizophrenic's oxygen consumption, cerebral circulation, and glucose prodution, for example, are common. Investigators also have reported detecting traces of toxic chemicals in the schizophrenic's blood as well as in his brain.

One group of studies, stimulated by speculations on the action of adrenalin, provides an example of the type of thinking that underlies the work of psychiatric biologists. Adrenalin, a naturally occurring hormone, has been theoretically implicated in a number of psychological disturbances. Referred to as the alarm chemical, it increases blood pressure and heart rate and is generally linked to states of arousal.

The specific association of adrenalin and schizophrenia was based on the observation that adrenalin's chemical structure resembles that of mescaline, an hallucinogenic drug derived from peyote. Scientists, therefore, reasoned that some byproduct of adrenalin metabolism might also produce hallucinations—and schizophrenia. Thus, the "adrenalin hypothesis" states that schizophrenia is the product of faulty adrenalin metabolism, which, in turn, causes the production of hallucinogenic body substances.

The adrenalin hypothesis is based on the fact that psychological stress generates large amounts of adrenalin. In normals, excess adrenalin is broken down into harmless, oxidized substances that the body then disposes of naturally. In schizophrenia, it is believed that the oxidation process is interfered with. As a result, the excess adrenalin is converted into *adrenochrome* and *adrenolutin*, two chemicals with alleged hallucinogenic properties. These subsequently enter the brain to produce the perceptual distortion and disorganization that is characteristic of schizophrenic disturbances.

Preliminary research tended to support the adrenalin hypothesis. Researchers reported that adrenalin was improperly metabolized in schizophrenics and that the amount of adrenochrome in the blood of normals increased upon administration of hallucinogenic substances such as LSD-25. Subsequent findings, however, produced quite a different picture. In one study, the rates of adrenalin destruction in normals and schizophrenics were shown not to differ. In another, researchers using highly sensitive techniques were not able to detect adrenochrome in the blood of any of their subjects, schizophrenic or otherwise. Finally, investigators were able to produce wide variations in adrenalin oxidation (reaching abnormal levels) simply by altering the level of Vitamin C in the body; deviations in the rate of adrenalin metabolism therefore seemed to be related more to diet than to schizophrenia.

Negative findings such as these were not isolated. In one instance after another, early indications of disordered biochemistry in schizophrenia turned out to be grossly exaggerated. Enthusiastic claims were invariably followed by negative or conflicting findings. Careful analysis revealed that most of the early biochemical studies did not take into account the effects of prolonged institutionalization. The schizophrenic patients in these studies had histories of dietary insufficiencies, infection, and extensive drug treatment. Investigators failed to realize that such factors could cause tremendous differences in blood serum tests and urine analyses.

To correct errors such as these, and to provide a perspective on the many breakthroughs claimed by biochemical investigators, a major research project was undertaken by the National Institute of Mental Health in 1956. The results of the project cast serious doubt on most of the findings that were previously reported, attributing them to poor hygienic standards, inadequate diets, and other factors. One of the studies, for example, showed that a chemical found earlier in the urine of schizophrenics was a metabolite of coffee and related more to coffee drinking than to mental illness. This substance was concentrated in the urine of schizophrenics simply because they spent a great deal of time sitting around hospital day rooms drinking coffee.

The biochemical findings, in sum, have turned out either to be negative or inconclusive. Seymour Kety, an NIMH scientist reviewing the overall outcome of his agency's project, comments, ". . . our schizophrenic patients, individually or as a group have shown little abnormality in the biological studies which have thus far been completed" (1959, p. 1530). Research in this area, nevertheless, continues, rooted in the conviction that positive findings in the genetic area must have biochemical correlates.

### The Sociological Perspective

The sociological approach to the study of schizophrenia attempts to transcend individual psychology and focuses instead on broader societal variables such as cross-cultural and socioeconomic differences. In historical perspective, much of the sociological theorizing regarding mental illness began with the hypothesis that civilization caused people to become mentally disturbed. The stresses and strains of bureaucracy and technology suposedly placed a terrific burden on a great number of people, causing some to break down. Research conducted over the years has since shown this to be a gross oversimplification. Most major disturbances found in bureaucratic, industrial societies are also found in primitive cultures. In fact, certain syndromes have been uncovered in less technological societies that are not found in our own. Two of these syndromes, Amok and Windigo, have been the subjects of intensive study.

*Amok* is a psychosis seen in Malaya, the Philippines, and various parts of Africa. The disorder begins with extended periods of depression and withdrawal, but progresses from there into a more dangerous phase. The afflicted person, for no apparent reason, is suddenly seized by murderous impulses that he cannot control. Grabbing a dagger, he screams wildly and slashes at anything or anyone in sight. Unless quickly subdued, the patient may harm or kill those about him; failing in this, he may mutilate himself. It is from this disorder that we get the phrase "running amok."

*Windigo*, a psychosis observed among Canadian Eskimos, also begins with protracted periods of depression. In the course of the disorder, the patient comes to believe that he is possessed by a "windigo," a supernatural ice giant who supposedly devours humans. Persons possessed by the windigo worry that they too will become cannibalistic and, as a result, suffer from insomnia, loss of appetite, and feelings of isolation. Some, however, get so disturbed that they ultimately murder and cannibalize members of their household.

Syndromes such as Amok and Windigo are quite rare and seem to be restricted to only certain cultures. Most of the more common psychoses, such as depression and schizophrenia, are distributed quite liberally among the nations of the world. Nevertheless, the precise nature of specific symptoms is likely to be related to cultural influences. Delusions and hallucinations, for example, often vary as a function of a patient's nationality or religion. Americans tend to incorporate FBI and CIA agents in their delusions while English and Russian patients implicate Scotland Yard and the KGB. Hallucinating Catholics and Protestants insist they hear the voice of Jesus, while Moslems hear the voice of Allah. The direction a patient's symptoms take obviously is a function of the culture to which he belongs.

Investigations into the relationship between sociological factors and mental illness center not only on cross-cultural differences but on differences within a culture as well. There thus are a number of studies relating variations in rates of mental illness to religious affiliation, native vs. immigrant status, and other variables of this sort. Two of the most well known *intracultural* studies have focused upon differences in societal disorganization and differences in social class. In both cases, the findings regarding schizophrenia have been especially revealing.

In the late 1930s, Faris and Dunham (1939) undertook to study whether personal disorganization (mental illness) was tied to social disorganization. Working in Chicago, they began with the fact that the greatest amount of social disorganization was concentrated in the inner city ghettos. In these areas we find the highest rates of broken homes, unemployment, and delinquency—standard indices of social disruption. If the "personal disorganization-social disorganization" hypothesis is correct, one should find the highest rates of mental disorders in these areas as well.

To test this hypothesis, Faris and Dunham divided a map of Chicago into concentric zones emanating from the downtown area and extending into the suburbs. The admission rates for mental patients were subsequently collected from hospitals throughout the city and tabulated for each zone.

The results are depicted in Figure 12. As can be seen, rates of mental illness are highest in the center city and diminish as one moves to outlying areas. Areas characterized by high rates of social disorganization therefore contain the highest rates of mental illness.

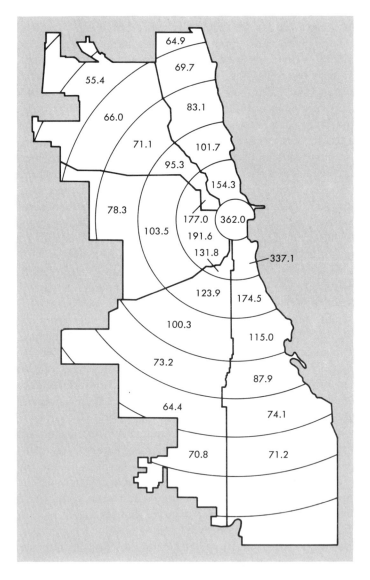

FIGURE 12.   Map of Chicago showing mental illness rates. From Faris and Dunham (1939, p. 36).

A breakdown of the various psychotic syndromes reveals an interesting pattern. The distribution of rates for schizophrenia approximates that found for mental illness in general; they are highest in the center city and decrease as one moves toward the periphery. Manic and depressive psychoses, however, are distributed randomly throughout the various zones. It thus appears that schizophrenia, more than the other psychoses, results from the disorganization associated with ghetto life.

However, some workers in the area suggest that schizophrenia contributes to, rather than results from, social disorganization. They contend that people who are severely disturbed drift to the ghetto either because they are rejected by family members or because they hope that center city living will place fewer demands on them. Since they are concentrated in the ghettos, they contribute to the high rates of delinquency, unemployment, and mental illness. This concept is referred to as the *downward drift* hypothesis. It essentially proposes that mental illness is the cause rather than the result of social disorganization. While an intriguing possibility, the downward drift hypothesis has received little empirical support. Most studies, including the one we turn to next, reveal that schizophrenic patients tend to stay in the same neighborhoods in which they grow up. The selective migration needed to support the downward drift hypothesis does not occur.

Hollingshead and Redlich (1958), following the path marked by Faris and Dunham, analyzed the relationship between mental disorder and *social class*. Specifically, they were interested in whether social position had a bearing on the *type of disorder* a person developed as well as the *type of psychiatric treatment* he received. For their target community, they chose New Haven, Connecticut.

Relying on standard indices of socioeconomic status such as area of residence, occupation, and education, Hollingshead and Redlich assigned subjects in their New Haven sample to one of five social classes. Class I was comprised of professionals and executives, people who make the most money, have the most education, and occupy most of the important leadership positions in the community. Class V, the lowest socioeconomic class, contained semiskilled factory hands and unskilled laborers. Individuals in this category typically have not gone beyond sixth grade and live either in cold water tenements or in outlying semirural slums. The characteristics of the remaining classes fall somewhere between these two, with the middle class represented by Class III.

The first major question Hollingshead and Redlich posed constitutes the basis for their entire investigation: Is class position related to mental illness? Using standard sampling techniques, they computed the frequency of psychiatric patients in each of the five socioeconomic classes. The data indicated that Class I contributed the least number, and Class V the greatest

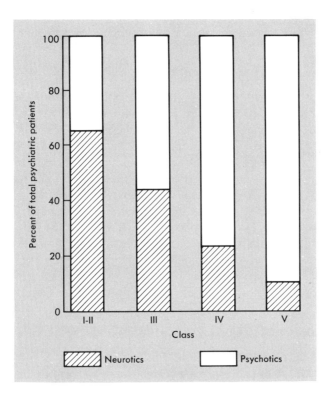

FIGURE 13.    Percentages of neurotics and psychotics in each social class. From Hollingshead and Redlich (1958, p. 223).

number, of mental patients. The relationship between social class and mental illness was clearly and unequivocally demonstrated.

The authors then inquired as to whether social class was related to *type* of diagnosis one receives. They divided their sample into neurotics and psychotics and calculated the relative proportion of each within the various classes. The results are depicted in Figure 13. Once again, a clearcut relationship emerges. Most neurotics are clustered in Classes I and II (combined in the graph for statistical reasons), while most psychotics fall into Class V. The psychiatric category a patient falls within is also related to his social class.

We should note that in referring to psychotics we are primarily speaking of schizophrenics since the greater proportion of psychotic patients receive this diagnosis. A separate analysis on schizophrenic patients verifies, even accentuates, the relationship between diagnosis and social class. Nine times as many schizophrenics are found in Class V than in Classes I and II combined!

## Table 5

*Principal Types of Therapy Received by Neurotic and Psychotic Patients*

| TYPE OF THERAPY ADMINISTERED | DIAGNOSIS OF PATIENTS | |
|---|---|---|
| | *% Neurotic* | *% Psychotic* |
| Psychotherapy | 82.9 | 16.4 |
| Organic Therapy | 11.1 | 38.8 |
| Custodial Care | 6.0 | 44.8 |

From Hollingshead and Redlich (1958).

Regarding treatment, the question arises whether one's diagnosis influences the type of psychiatric care he receives. Hollingshead and Redlich addressed themselves to this question by first breaking down treatment possibilities into three separate categories: psychotherapy, organic treatment, and custodial care. Psychotherapy encompasses individual and group approaches to behavior change based on discussion and re-education. Organic treatment includes lobotomies (brain surgery) in addition to various types of shock treatments. Custodial care simply involves keeping a patient institutionalized and is functionally equivalent to no treatment at all.

The authors computed the number of neurotic and psychotic patients who received each type of treatment; the results are shown in Table 5. It is evident that the overwhelming majority of psychotic patients, most of whom are schizophrenic and poor, receive less preferential treatment, if they receive any treatment at all. Neurotic patients, most of whom are in the upper classes, are the ones who receive psychotherapy.

The New Haven study, in sum, corroborates earlier findings in which mental illness and class status were shown to be associated. But it also demonstrates quite convincingly that a patient's diagnosis as well as the treatment he receives are also tied to social class. To the extent that social factors, psychopathology, and treatment are so intertwined, it becomes necessary to explore in more depth the ways society views and deals with mental illness. This is the task we have set for ourselves in the next chapter.

# The Societal Response to Abnormal Behavior

## chapter four

In order to provide its citizens with a sense of security and order, every society develops ways of dealing with deviance. Our society is no different. In the case of the criminal, for example, our society uses punishment; in the case of the mentally ill, we depend upon treatment. The ostensible goal in both instances is rehabilitation. However, treatment of the mentally ill is unfortunately often indistinguishable from punishment, and rehabilitation is little more than an empty promise.

In this chapter we will examine the procedures and devices our society uses to deal with the mentally ill. We begin by looking at the treatment of disturbed individuals in the hospitals and courts, the institutions that deal most intimately with the mentally ill.

### The Mental Hospital

Although the notion of hospitalization for the mentally ill can be traced to the Aesculapian temples of ancient Greece, it had its true beginnings in late eighteenth-century Europe. At about the same time Pinel was freeing the Bicetre inmates from their chains, a wealthy English Quaker named

William Tuke established the first sanctuary, or asylum, for the mentally ill. It was named the York Retreat, to avoid the negative connotations of the word "asylum," and offered mental patients a place to rest and recuperate. Tuke's approach to the treatment of the mentally ill proved highly successful, and word of his success spread rapidly.

However, despite a promising beginning, most mental patients (particularly the poor) continued to be treated dismally, especially in America where patients were interred in local jails and poorhouses. In the mid-nineteenth century, a retired school teacher named Dorothea Dix began to campaign for the humanitarian treatment of the mentally ill, a campaign that lasted approximately forty years. Biographical accounts of her career credit her with helping to establish over thirty state mental hospitals.

Dorothea Dix's pioneering work resulted in many revolutionary reforms, not the least of which was the replacement of crowded jails and almshouses with well-staffed hospitals. As time passed, however, the shortcomings of the state mental hospital system became increasingly evident. First, construction of mental institutions in outlying regions isolated the patient from his freinds and family. Second, the local community's sense of obligation for its disturbed members lessened as the state assumed major responsibility for their care. Finally, institutional life itself seemed to contribute elements that interfered with the process of recovery.

Erving Goffman, a sociologist who has studied institutions in some depth, offers a penetrating analysis on the workings of mental hospitals. In *Asylums* (1961), he characterizes mental hospitals as "total institutions," places in which inmate activity is highly regimented and constantly under the watchful eye of the resident staff. The most salient characteristic of a total institution, Goffman points out, is the handling of many human needs through the bureaucratic manipulation of large blocks of people. Under such circumstances, the needs and desires of the individual become subordinated to the smooth and troublefree operation of the institution. In large mental hospitals, individual concerns are relegated to a secondary status and patient management becomes of prime importance.

The major forms of patient management are the hospital's ward system and the coercive use of certain types of "therapy." Within the ward system, patients are assigned to open or closed (locked) wards as a function of their diagnosis or the severity of their disorder. Segregation of this sort is justified on the grounds that it is done for the patient's benefit; the patient on the closed ward is provided with controls and the opportunity to receive round-the-clock attention from the professional help. The therapeutic rationale for the ward system, however, is belied by the fact that the closed and typically most troublesome wards are staffed by the least proficient members of the staff. The patients who need help most are placed in the care of those least capable of providing it. The ward system, in essence, functions merely as an institutional device to handle recalcitrant patients.

Many hospitals, in addition, rely on sedative drugs and seclusion as a means of managing unruly inmates. The ways in which these are disguised as therapy have been described by those who have studied hospital practices. In *Human Problems of a State Mental Hospital* (1956), Belknap writes:

> When any patient is rude or insubordinate to the attendants or to a worker carrying out the attendant's orders, or when the patient picks a fight with another patient or becomes violently aggressive in general, he may be placed in one of the ward seclusion rooms, or special cells. In theory, this seclusion is carried out by the attendant and his lieutenants for the patient's own good and to give him an opportunity to cool off. But in most cases of disturbance we witnessed this was not exactly the spirit in which the patient was incarcerated. In addition to its outright use in ward discipline for unruly patients, the threat of seclusion was often employed by the attendants or working patients to secure discipline. (p. 191)

A similar observation is made by Stanton and Schwartz in their classic study, *The Mental Hospital* (1954). After discussing the controversial ways attendants control patients through the manipulation of "ground privileges," they note:

> Seclusion,* cold wet sheet packs,† and sedative medications were similarly controversial because they, too, were ambiguous. All were prescribed officially as "treatment" which was to be given to a patient only when expected to be beneficial for him. But at the same time, all were used also as measures of social restraint, despite continuous assertions that they were "treatment, not punishment" by persons high in the hierarchy. These assertions were ignored for the simple reason that they were not always true; out of context, they were merely confusing. (p. 127)

> * Seclusion is the term denoting a patient's being locked alone in his room. Although according to the law in some states the term does not include the locking in of patients for the night, this meaning is included in the word as used at the hospital, and in this account.
> † A hydrotherapeutic measure: patients are wrapped closely in cold wet sheets; after a few minutes, the patient becomes flushed and warm, he is quieted and often goes to sleep. However, if the patient objects to the measure, the sedative effect is much less likely to occur. Cold packs clearly can be used easily as a substitute for simple restraint.

It should be noted that the institution studied by Stanton and Schwartz is considered to be one of the foremost mental hospitals in the country.

This rather bleak state of affairs is compounded by the fact that most mental institutions have limited resources for providing psychological treatment. Some hospitals are so severely understaffed that psychiatrists may spend only a few minutes a week with a patient, if that much; psychotherapy in most large mental hospitals is virtually non-existent. Whatever therapy patients receive usually falls into the category of organic treatment, a phrase used to denote psychosurgery, shock treatment, and medication by drugs.

Psychosurgery refers to certain forms of brain surgery first used in the 1930s. Although a number of surgical techniques were developed in this period (see Figure 14), prefrontal lobotomy was the most common. This operation involved severing the neural tracts between the thalamus, thought to be the center of emotionality, and the frontal lobes, the supposed intellectual centers. The apparent purpose of this operation was to keep the patient's emotional disturbance from interfering with his rational thought processes. As simplistic as this notion may have been, it formed the basis for thousands of such operations. Psychosurgery has grown out of vogue in recent years because of the increased availability of psychiatric drugs. It nevertheless continues to be used in isolated instances.

Shock treatment, in contrast, is a technique that is still used fairly extensively. Although several types of shock treatment exist, the most com-

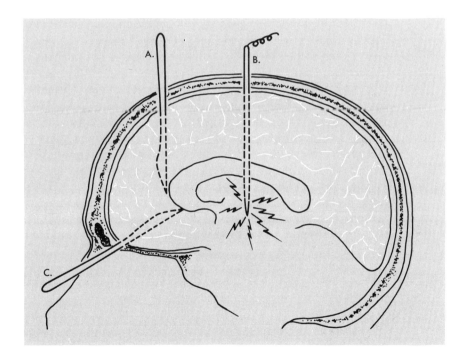

FIGURE 14.   Forms of psychosurgery: *A*, standard "prefrontal" lobotomy; *B*, thalamotomy (destruction of portions of the thalamus by electrical current); *C*, transorbital lobotomy (prefrontal lobotomy using cranial cavity above the eyes as entry).

mon form is Electro-Convulsive Therapy (ECT). In ECT, electrodes are pressed against the patient's temples and an electric current passed through his brain. This causes a momentary convulsion followed by a brief period in which the patient feels groggy and disoriented. In the early days of ECT (the 1930's and 1940's), some patients suffered fractured spines from the convulsive movements caused by the electric current. Today, a curare-type drug is administered beforehand to produce temporary paralysis and reduce the risk of physical injury. While ECT seems to have beneficial effects with certain patients, particularly those suffering from depression, its effects tend to be relatively shortlived. It is nevertheless employed in cases where drugs do not seem to work.

The use of chemical substances to treat mental illness is known as *chemotherapy*, with specific agents referred to as *psychoactive* drugs. These drugs, for the most part, consist of *tranquilizers* and *antidepressants*. Tranquilizers are used to allay anxiety and reduce irritability, and are most effective in cases of schizophrenia and severe neuroses. The antidepressants, or energizers as they sometimes are called, are primarily employed to combat depression; however, they may be used to treat any syndrome characterized by withdrawal and apathy.

The universal acceptance of the psychoactive drugs, beginning with their introduction in the early 1950's, has resulted in their widespread use. This has had a tremendous impact on the treatment of the mentally ill and has led to the release of patients who might not otherwise have been discharged. The wholesale use of drugs, nevertheless, has its negative side; a great many psychiatrists have come to rely upon chemotherapy as a treatment in itself even though it clearly was not meant to be used in this way. Drugs were originally designed to be used in conjunction with psychotherapy in cases of severely disturbed patients who could not be approached in any other way. But this consideration has been repeatedly overlooked; most patients in mental hospitals are treated with drugs and nothing else.

The use of biological treatment techniques in our mental institutions is often justified on the grounds that they are quick, easy to administer, and act to free valuable psychiatric time. This argument tends to mask the fact that the wholesale use of these techniques reflects the ubiquitous presence of the organic model in the operating philosophy of mental hospitals. In a great many instances, this helps to develop and reinforce deeply ingrained attitudes of incurability, attitudes that perpetuate the operation of those psychological graveyards euphemistically labeled "chronic services" or "continued treatment wards."

Treatment of the mentally ill within our mental hospitals, in sum, leaves little room for pride or optimism. We might nevertheless point out that some changes are taking place. In recent years there has been a movement toward "open" hospitals where there are no locked wards, where "ground privileges" are a right rather than a reward. These use milieu therapy and patient government, relying on the patient's daily activities rather than once-a-week contact with a psychiatrist as the medium for psychotherapeutic change. But these changes are few and far between. In most large state mental institutions, patients are treated solely by ECT and drugs and receive little personal attention. Many of these patients display chronic recidivism patterns and are unable to stay out of the hospital for any length of time.

J. K. Wing, a British researcher interested in the consequences of long-term institutionalization, sought to discover what effect extended hospital stays have on a patient's wish to be released (1962). Working with a group of schizophrenics who had been institutionalized for periods ranging up to twenty years, he divided them into subgroups according to their length of stay. Data consisting of symptom ratings, attitudes toward discharge, and plans for the future were collected for each group and subjected to analysis.

The major finding of this study is strikingly depicted in Figure 15. The longer a patient stays in the hospital, the more apathetic he gets about outside life and the more unwilling he is to leave the institution. Further

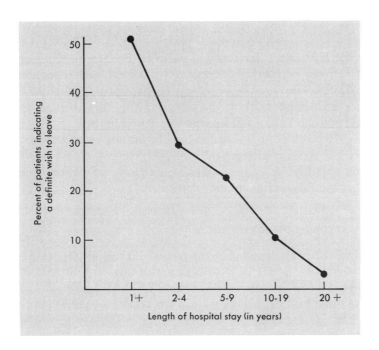

FIGURE 15. Attitudes toward discharge as a function of length of hospital stay. After Wing (1962).

examination of Figure 15 indicates that after only two years in the hospital, fewer than thirty percent of the patients show a desire to leave. The majority of the patients either wish to stay or show marked apathy.

Wing called the mental patient's gradual aversion towards civilian life *institutionalism*. Aversion of this sort is characterized by deterioration in social skills, a rejection of social activities, and a pervasive loss of initiative. At the root of the institutionalism syndrome is the diminished sense of personal responsibility that hospital life tends to foster. When one's feeding, bathing, dressing, and recreational activities are all scheduled and monitored by others, life reduces to little more than a series of automated movements. Eventually the patient stops caring and starts being cared for.

If the mental patient's status is ever to be improved, either a substitute for mental hospitals must be found or mental hospitals must truly become treatment centers. If the second alternative is adopted, smaller hospitals with reasonable doctor-to-patient ratios must become the rule rather than the exception. Furthermore, radically different treatment approaches may have to be developed for patients with radically different needs. We discuss some of the innovations that bear on these considerations later in this chapter under the heading of Community Mental Health.

## The Courts

The mental patient is subjected to the legal machinery of society for different reasons; he may be the focus of a commitment proceeding to hospitalize him against his will, or he may be charged with committing a crime. If he is accused of a crime, the central issue is whether he ought to be brought to trial, and, if so, whether he should be held responsible for his actions. Regardless of the particular circumstances, questions arise concerning the rights and legal status of the mentally ill. We consider some of these questions under the separate headings of involuntary commitment, the right to trial, and the insanity defense.

### INVOLUNTARY COMMITMENT

Individuals who spend time in mental hospitals may arrive there by different routes. Some, acknowledging that they are ill and in need of help, voluntarily request to be committed. They may stay for varying periods of time and can usually leave whenever they desire. Others, failing to realize the extent of their disturbance, may have to be hospitalized involuntarily. For these individuals, discharge from a mental institution is not so simple; in large hospitals where many patients are delusional, it is often difficult for a legally committed mental patient to convince others that he has recovered and that his claim to health is legitimate. The danger of unjustified long-term incarceration is therefore very real.

Since the implications of involuntary hospitalization are not to be taken lightly, it is imperative that commitment proceedings be conducted with utmost care. Over the years, a number of elaborate safeguards have been set up to protect the rights of the mentally ill. In practice, however, such safeguards are deftly sidestepped or ignored. As a result, there is a wide chasm between what the legal statutes stipulate and what occurs in the courtroom.

Several studies have taken a close look at what actually happens in commitment proceedings. Kutner (1962) studied the practice of requiring psychiatric examinations before trial. He found that while the courts do follow the letter of the law in appointing doctors to conduct psychiatric examinations, most of these examinations are completed in only two or three minutes. This is hardly enough time to conduct a serious psychiatric investigation. Kutner also reports that in these proceedings, patients are practically never informed of their right to an attorney. The result is that they are represented only by their relatives—those who usually institute the commitment proceedings in the first place!

In an investigation with a similar focus, Scheff (1964) offers support for Kutner's findings. After carefully comparing commitment proceedings in rural and urban courts, he concludes that the overwhelming majority serve no serious investigatory purpose. The commitment proceedings in most of the urban courts he examined (where the largest volume of cases are processed) were largely ceremonial in nature and lasted an average of only seven minutes. Once a patient was brought into court, his commitment was practically assured.

Officials involved in these hearings justify what goes on by claiming that it spares the patient the anguish of long drawn-out proceedings. They also maintain that involuntary commitment leads to effective psychiatric treatment and can do no harm. One need not probe this position too deeply to prove that it is untenable; we have already seen that effective psychiatric treatment in most mental hospitals is a myth. Furthermore, there is evidence that involuntary hospitalization can adversely affect one's future relationship with employers and friends. Arguing that commitment can do no harm is at best naive and based more on wishful thinking than on sociological evidence.

For obvious reasons, involuntary commitment is necessary in some cases. The patient may be dangerous to himself or to others, or be completely unaware that he is seriously disturbed. Nevertheless, some legal experts advocate abolishing enforced hospitalization on the grounds that its benefits do not outweigh its dangers. A less drastic alternative would be to simply bring current legal practice into line with existing legal statutes and to make sure that commitment proceedings are conducted more seriously. Unless this can be accomplished, involuntary commitment will become increasingly indefensible.

## THE RIGHT TO TRIAL

One of the basic foundations of modern law is the right of every criminally-charged individual to trial by jury. This guarantee, however, does not always apply to persons who are deemed psychologically disturbed by the courts. When this occurs, the individual's status under the law changes drastically, and his right to trial may be legally denied. This is illustrated in the following excerpt.

> LOS ANGELES
>
> Charles "Tex" Watson, a tall Texan slated to stand trial alone in the murder of actress Sharon Tate and six others, was committed to a mental institution Friday. . . .
>
> Watson, 24, a clean-cut looking young man, has been described at the trial of Charles Manson and three women members of Manson's hippie-style clan as the leader of killer parties that killed Miss Tate and the six others.
>
> He fought extradition from Texas until after the trial of the others began. Since arriving, he has stood silent, with mouth agape, occasionally smiling aimlessly, in several court appearances. . . .
>
> A report by a psychiatrist, Dr. Marcus Crahan, said: "Mr. Watson in the last week has become listless, flacid (sic), and makes no movements. . . ."
>
> Another psychiatrist, Dr. Seymour Pollack, told the court Watson could not cooperate with an attorney as he refuses to speak. . . .
>
> Judge Dell ordered him moved immediately to Atascadero State Hospital and declared, "he is not capable of understanding at this time the nature of the charges against him. I feel it is imperative that he be placed in a facility where he may be able to regain his sanity." (Associated Press Release, *Springfield Union*, October 31, 1970)

The law insists that defendants be capable of aiding in their own defense; not only must they display interest in their personal welfare but they must be able to provide information to help their attorneys. Many disturbed individuals, in the eyes of the law, are incapable of cooperation or self-concern and are therefore judged incompetent to stand trial, as seen above.

Thomas Szasz, author of *Law, Liberty, and Psychiatry* (1963), vehemently criticizes the process of determining incompetency. Mental patients charged with criminal acts, he argues, are repeatedly placed in jeopardy by what he sees as questionable legal procedures. A great many court-appointed psychiatrists, for example, do not fully explain their role vis-à-vis the court to their "clients." Defendants often unwittingly assume that whatever they reveal will remain confidential and will not be used against them, and may disclose information that can prove self-incriminating. Since the constitution is meant to protect against the unauthorized use of self-incriminating evidence, such pretrial examinations constitute a form of mind-tapping (Szasz, p. 161).

Perhaps more damaging is the fact that incompetency rulings are tantamount to indefinite jail sentences. When a patient is found incompetent, he is automatically committed to a mental hospital, usually a hospital for the criminally insane, and has to stay there until he is deemed ready to stand trial. Defendants who enter such hospitals, however, rarely receive treatment and may spend their entire lives, or at least a significant portion of them, under lock and key.

Although Tex Watson, the defendant in the preceding excerpt, was ultimately judged competent to stand trial, cases in which such outcomes occur are more the exception than the rule. In a recent study of over one thousand defendants committed to a state hospital in Michigan over a six-year period, it was found that only ten percent were ever returned to trial (Hess and Thomas, 1963). The authors of the study indicate that most of these defendants could have been returned to the courts in short periods of time had they been represented by interested attorneys. They estimate that over fifty percent of the institutionalized defendants would spend the rest of their lives in the hospital.

To vividly illustrate what can happen as a result of an ill-considered competency ruling, Szasz points to the case of Ezra Pound, the famous poet. During World War II, Pound allegedly made treasonous broadcasts against the Allies while living in Italy. In 1945, after the war was over, he was arrested and tried for treason. Pound always claimed that his broadcasts were born of patriotism and insisted that he might have prevented the war if he had been able to send his messages to the enemy prior to 1940. It is unimportant here to debate whether in fact Pound's actions were treasonous; the issue is that the question was never debated in court.

Whether Pound's broadcasts were or were not treasonous was, however, never decided. That is, the issue and the evidence on it were never presented to a jury. Hence, no judicial decision on his guilt or innocence was ever rendered. Instead, it was decided—jointly by the government and by Pound's defense—that Pound be declared mentally unfit to stand trial and that he be hospitalized in a psychiatric institution. This was speedily accomplished. It took the jury all of three minutes to decide that Pound was of "unsound mind." He spent the next 13 years in St. Elizabeth's Hospital. (Szasz, 1963, p. 200)

At the urging of Robert Frost and other prominent literary figures, the government eventually dropped its indictment against Pound in 1958. But not, as the excerpt indicates, until thirteen years of hospitalization had elapsed.

A number of people, including Szasz, strongly maintain that disturbed individuals should be made to face trial, arguing that most defendants are capable of defining their own interests. According to Szasz, judgments of incompetency are used much too widely and often depend on arbitrary rulings by unsophisticated judges. He contends that it would be more charitable to try a disturbed person and provide him with psychological treatment in jail (if found guilty) than it is to deprive him of his right to be tried. Since depriving a person of this right ostensibly results in imprisonment anyway, it cannot be justified on therapeutic grounds nor on the basis of humane considerations.

THE INSANITY DEFENSE

We have considered what happens to those accused of a crime but regarded as incompetent to stand trial. We turn now to criminal defendants who are able to comprehend a judicial proceeding but claim they were "out of their minds" *while the crime was committed*. This is the classic insanity defense, commonly referred to as the "temporary insanity" plea.

Insanity as a defense dates back to an incident that occurred over a hundred years ago in Great Britain. In 1843, Daniel M'Naghten tried to shoot and kill Sir Robert Peel, the English Prime Minister, whom he believed to be plotting against him. Although the shot missed Peel, it killed Peel's private secretary and M'Naghten was charged with murder. Insanity was the defense and, after a hardfought trial, the jury brought in a verdict of not guilty on the ground of insanity. M'Naghten was subsequently committed to Bethlehem Hospital where he spent the last 22 years of his life.

This revolutionary verdict led the judges of England to formulate the criteria for future acquittals based on insanity. The result of their deliberations, referred to as the "M'Naghten rule," states:

> to establish a defense on the ground of insanity, it must be clearly proved that, at the time of committing the act, the party accused was labouring under such a defect of reason, from disease of the mind, as not to know the nature and quality of the act he was doing, or if he did know it, that he did not know he was doing what was wrong.

To understand the meaning of the M'Naghten rule, we must remember that laws are primarily designed to punish those who *willfully* commit crimes. The legal statutes consequently contain provisions for cases of accident or negligence. Under circumstances of this sort, referred to as "excusing conditions," punishment is either mitigated or eliminated. The M'Naghten rule set a legal precedent by placing insanity in the category of an excusing condition.

For nearly a hundred years, the M'Naghten rule functioned as the sole test of legal responsibility in criminal cases involving the mentally ill. The contribution of psychiatry, however, remained relatively limited. Psychiatrists were only allowed to offer an opinion on the patient's ability to distinguish right from wrong. They could not elaborate on the patient's motives or capacity to control himself. The M'Naghten rule, in many cases, did not further the cause of the disturbed client since testimony regarding the psychological nature of his disturbance was barred.

In 1954, as a result of a decision handed down by the United States Court of Appeals, the definition of the M'Naghten rule was reinterpreted. In the case of Durham v. U. S., the court ruled that "an accused is not criminally responsible if his unlawful act was the product of mental disease or mental defect." The Durham decision broadened the definition of an excusing condition, allowing psychiatrists and psychologists to present to the court more relevant material regarding the patient's disturbance. Since its inception, the decision has been widely acclaimed by members of both the legal and psychiatric profession.

However, the Durham rule has not solved all the problems associated with the prosecution of disturbed individuals. First, not all states have put the rule into practice. Second, the Durham rule, like its predecessor, the M'Naghten rule, still often results in the misleading and fallacious verdict of "acquittal by reason of insanity." Rulings of this sort are contradictory since they simply do not result in acquittal. In practically every case where a verdict of this type is reached, the defendant is automatically committed to a hospital for the criminally insane. Hospitals of this sort, as indicated earlier, are nothing less than prisons. "The defendant, sentenced to a prison disguised as a hospital, receives no treatment, but is nevertheless expected to remain there until cured" (Szasz, 1963, p. 114). In practice, many offenders spend more time in detention when "acquitted" than they would had they been found guilty and forced to serve the maximum sentence.

The use of indeterminate, or open-ended, sentencing is viewed by many to be a form of cruel and unusual punishment. It is contrary to the basic tenets of modern criminal justice where the severity of punishment is supposed to be related to the severity of the crime. The British, in an attempt to reduce the probability of unjustified imprisonment, have adopted the "guilty but mentally ill" sentence. Under this sentence, a guilty defendant can, at the court's discretion, still be sent to a mental institution. He may not, however, be kept there beyond the maximum sentence he would have received had he been sent to prison. By invoking this alternative, some of the evils of indeterminate sentencing are thus avoided.

In summary, we conclude that the mentally ill receive less than adequate treatment in their encounters with the courts. Whatever consideration is accorded them in the legal statutes is often ignored in the day-to-day practice of the law. The psychologically disturbed citizen, whether he appears in the civil or criminal courts, is apt to be deprived of his rights and robbed of his dignity. In this regard, he is treated no differently by the courts than he is by the mental hospital.

What types of social forces are responsible for these conditions? The answer lies partially in the limitations and pressures associated with the operation of societal agencies; the courts and the mental hospitals are so overextended that overcrowded court dockets and long hospital waiting lists are common. Another part of the answer lies in the fact that many public agencies are staffed with low caliber professionals. The most highly skilled members of the legal and psychiatric professions are usually found in private practice or working for private institutions, not in public agencies. But the entire responsibility cannot be placed solely at the doors of these agencies. We must also consider the attitudes and reactions of the general public.

### The Public

Studying the man-in-the-street's reaction to something as complex as mental illness is not an easy task. The things that people publicly admit on questionnaires often differ quite markedly from what they actually believe. Taking this into consideration, Jum Nunnally set out to assess the public's view of mental illness in a study entitled *Popular Conceptions of Mental Health* (1961). To accurately appraise the true character of these conceptions, he decided to separately assess the public's *information* about mental illness and contrast this with *attitudes* toward the same topic. The extent of factual information regarding mental illness was obtained by a questionnaire containing statements on the topic. Respondents were required to indicate the extent to which they agreed or disagreed with such items as:

> Most of the people in mental hospitals speak in words that can be understood.
> There is not much that can be done for a person who develops a mental disorder.
> Most people who "go crazy" try to kill themselves.
> Few of the people who seek psychiatric help need the treatment.

Attitudes were measured by the Semantic Differential (Osgood, Suci, and Tannenbaum, 1957), a test that measures underlying feelings more than actual information. The subject is given a stimulus word and required to rate it on a number of evaluative dimensions. An example of a test item for the word "Psychiatrist" is given below:

### PSYCHIATRIST

```
  Ignorant____ : ____ : ____ : ____ : ____ : ____Intelligent
 Effective____ : ____ : ____ : ____ : ____ : ____Ineffective
     Weak____ : ____ : ____ : ____ : ____ : ____Strong
  Anxious____ : ____ : ____ : ____ : ____ : ____Calm
```

Semantic Differential items similar to this can be applied to other stimuli, such as, "mental patient," "average man," and so on.

The results of the two tests were quite revealing. On the information questionnaire, the mentally ill were portrayed quite positively. They were described as coherent, potentially curable, and capable of returning to their communities. Generally speaking, the public seemed to subscribe to an enlightened view of mental illness. But on the Semantic Differential, a rather different picture emerged. Here the mentally ill were regarded with fear and distrust, irrespective of a respondent's age or education. According to Nunnally, "Old people and young people, highly educated people and people with little formal schooling—all tend to regard the mentally ill as relatively dangerous, dirty, unpredictable, and worthless" (p. 51).

It is evident that the public's reaction to mental illness is very complex. The mentally ill are *publicly* spoken of in optimistic terms; unfortunate as they may be, they are depicted as dignified human beings capable of rehabilitation. On the other hand, they are *privately* regarded as fearsome aliens, as something less than human. Since the mental patient must ultimately contend with what people feel more than with what they say, we can only reach one conclusion: To be mentally ill is to be stigmatized.

Erving Goffman, in a book entitled *Stigma* (1963), addresses himself to the question of how the public deals with deviants. He takes as his starting point the fact that there are many different types of discrediting attributes than can lower a person's status. Generally speaking, these fall into three major categories: bodily, tribal, and characterological stigma. Bodily stigmata encompass a variety of physical anomalies, such as facial deformities and crippled limbs; *tribal* stigmata are direct indications of a person's race, religion, or nationality as reflected in facial features or skin color; *characterological* stigmata refer to blemishes of individual character, such as weak will, irresponsibility, and other psychological qualities usually associated with a past history of addiction, imprisonment, or mental illness.

The main concern of the stigmatized individual is depicted in the phrase: "interpersonal acceptance." Throughout his life he must learn to deal with people who are secretly repulsed by him, but who nevertheless insist upon maintaining a façade of benevolent tolerance. The stigmatized individual, Goffman implies, must learn to cope with the underlying attitude rather than with the façade if he is to insure his social survival.

The type of adjustment that a stigmatized individual settles upon depends somewhat on the visibility of his shortcoming. In cases of bodily stigma, and some instances of tribal stigma, one's handicap is usually obvious. It is not as obvious in most cases of characterological stigma.[3] Many ex-mental patients nevertheless still face a difficult choice. They may keep their status a secret and attempt to pass, or reveal their true identity and cope with the consequences.

The patient who decides to pass typically must resort to a series of complex interpersonal maneuvers in order to avoid detection. If at a party he hears a disparaging joke about disturbed individuals, he must laugh along with everyone else. If his acquaintances inadvertently throw about words like "kooky" or "crazy," he must be careful not to wince or get angry. A homosexual who tried to pass writes:

> When jokes were made about "queers" I had to laugh with the rest, and when talk was about women I had to invent conquests of my own. I hated myself at such moments, but there seemed to be nothing else that I could do. My whole life became a lie. . . .
>
> The strain of deceiving my family and friends often became intolerable. It was necessary for me to watch every word I spoke and every gesture I made in case I gave myself away. (Wildeblood, 1959, p. 32)

No matter how careful he is, the person who passes does so with the knowledge that his acceptance by others is unwitting. The same people who accept him are prejudiced against the type of person that he really is.

The patient who reveals his true identity also encounters difficulties. Unlike the patient who passes, he must constantly be concerned with reducing anxiety in normals, since normals, with few exceptions, feel ill at ease in the company of ex-mental patients. If, for example, things get sticky during a small group conversation, he may casually make a remark about the time he spent in the "nut house." Everyone laughs, relieved that he, not they, said it first. He may also go out of his way to assure people who carelessly use the words "nut" or "weirdo" in his presence that it really does not matter. Finally he may decide to bring up mental illness

---

[3] This, despite the mass media's depiction of mental patients as incoherent and glassy-eyed.

as a topic for serious discussion, a maneuver Goffman refers to as "disclosure etiquette." Whether a patient passes or reveals himself, he is forced to depend on calculated ploys to mitigate the effect of his stigma.

Must the stigmatized resort to such extreme maneuvers? Do people respond to the mentally ill as negatively as Goffman describes? Amerigo Farina, a psychologist working in this area, has addressed himself to these questions in a series of innovative laboratory studies. His general approach involves setting up a two-person experimental task in which each of the participants believes his partner to be an ex-mental patient. This allows Farina to behaviorally assess the ways in which people respond to persons whom they believe to be mentally ill.

In one study (Farina and Ring, 1965), Farina was interested in the effect an ex-mental patient would have on a partner with whom he had to work closely. Before the subjects actually began working with one another they were asked to write brief autobiographies on slips of paper and to share this background data with their partners. They handed the slips to the experimenter who passed them on to the appropriate party. In the exchange process, the experimenter secretly substituted new slips for half the subjects, leading both members of certain pairs to believe that their partners had been hospitalized in the past for a nervous breakdown. Pairs who went through this procedure comprised the "stigmatized" group. The background information slips that they received read as follows:

> You asked us to be candid, so here goes: I have certain problems in adjustment which I first noticed in high school and which still bother me quite a bit. I guess I am somewhat different from most people I tend to keep pretty much to myself and, frankly, I don't really have any close friends. At school I am doing pretty well (about a B average). I suppose what's most unusual about me is that twice (once in my senior year in high school and once in college), I have been placed in a mental institution when I had a kind of nervous breakdown. As for my goals for the future, after graduating from college, I hope to go to graduate school. (p. 48)

Another group of subjects went through essentially the same procedure with the exception that all references to a nervous breakdown was deleted from the background data. Their information slips read:

> I tend to think of myself as a relatively normal person; at least I don't have what you could call any "problems." I enjoy going to college, but like to have my fun, too. I think I'm pretty popular with my group, am engaged, and am doing pretty well (about a B average) in school. Frankly, I can't think of anything that's "unusual" about myself. As for my goals for the future, after graduating from college, I plan to get married and hope to go to graduate school. (p. 48)

These pairs constituted the "normal" or control group.

The experiment required pairs of participants to obtain as high a score as possible working on a task requiring joint participation. The task consisted of a mazelike contraption containing a steel ball, a number of holes, and two sets of controls, one for each subject. When operated jointly, the controls allowed the ball to be moved through the maze. The object of the task was to guide the ball as far through the maze as possible without letting it drop into a hole. The average distance covered over a series of trials constituted a partnership's score. Following completion of the task, all subjects were asked to fill out questionnaires regarding their perception of their co-workers. They were then informed of the experiment's true purpose and the reason for the manipulation.

The performance of the groups on the experimental task was unusual, but not entirely unexpected. Pairs comprised of "ex-mental patients," that is, stigmatized partners, did significantly *better* than the "normal" pairs. Farina reasoned that in tasks of this sort, it is *less threatening* to work with a person who is considered mentally ill since that person is in less of a position to be critical and judgmental. Working with a normal person, he contends, produces relatively more anxiety and results in poorer performance.

One could also argue that the better performance in the stigmatized group may have been a function of the participants' overcompensating for the perceived inadequacy of their "disturbed" co-workers. Regardless of why the task performance turned out the way it did, the questionnaire responses unequivocally indicated that stigmatized partners were held in low esteem. Subjects who believed that they were working with mentally ill co-workers indicated that they would have preferred to work alone. These subjects also described their partners as hindering their joint performance more often than subjects who believed they were working with normals. This occurred despite the fact that the stigmatized pairs performed better. We therefore see that the stigma associated with ex-mental patient status results in a negative interpersonal response even though the ex-patient's actual behavior in no way justifies it.

In other studies conducted by Farina and his colleagues, similar findings emerge. The ex-mental patient is invariably treated as if he were incompetent, unreliable, and inadequate. Generally speaking, the research evidence strongly supports what Goffman describes in the pages of *Stigma*. It can be concluded that the institutional plight of the mentally ill, as reflected in their treatment by the courts and the mental hospital, is just a part of a broader societal pattern signifying degradation and rejection.

Despite these conclusions, there are indications that efforts are being made to change things. The National Association for Mental Health, for example, carries on a perennial campaign to re-educate the public in the area of mental health. Under its auspices, advertising campaigns combat the myths about mental illness that the public finds so hard to relinquish. In addition, federal and state funds are periodically allocated to upgrade the conditions in existing institutions. But the major changes that are taking place are contained in the community mental health movement.

## Community Mental Health

The community mental health movement had its official beginnings in a report published by the Joint Commission for Mental Illness and Health. Distributed under the title of *Action for Mental Health* (1961), the report made sweeping recommendations regarding the future care of the mentally ill. Among the topics touched upon were large state mental hospitals, community based treatment centers, and the mental health manpower shortage. ·

In *Action for Mental Health*, large custodial mental institutions were subjected to careful and lengthy scrutiny; the result was a recommendation to abolish them. Existing institutions were to be converted into intensive treatment centers and the construction of any new state hospital of over 1000 beds was to be prohibited. The report also advised local communities to develop psychiatric units as integral parts of their general hospitals. These would be designed to offer intensive treatment and short term hospitalization for community residents.

The report, at the same time, strongly urged the widespread deployment of community mental health centers. Designed to offer both in-patient and out-patient care, these would provide treatment for disturbed individuals without requiring them to leave their usual surroundings. Patients, as a result, would be spared the inconvenience and adverse effects associated with extended stays in large mental institutions. Considering the ease with which patients slip into institutionalism patterns, the importance of this cannot be overemphasized.

One of the major benefits of community based treatment is that it allows the patient to maintain contact with people in the community who traditionally function as "care givers"—physicians, teachers, ministers, and other persons who often provide invaluable support in times of stress. Keeping the disturbed individual in his native surroundings, therefore, can play an important role in the recovery process. In addition, the community approach allows for the use of relatively novel treatment techniques, such as family and marital therapy, the success of which depends upon the active participation of family members.

One of the more ominous findings in the Joint Commission's report concerned the issue of mental health manpower. Very briefly, the report pointed to a dangerous deficiency in the number of mental health professionals currently in practice and indicated that matters would get increasingly worse. Before considering the commission's recommendations, it will be helpful to sketch out exactly who these professionals are and to briefly describe what they do.

The *clinical psychologist* specializes in work with the mentally ill. His training involves four to five years of graduate work at a university and results in a Ph.D. degree. As a graduate student, he receives a basic grounding in psychological theory and research along with exposure to clinical work. Practical experience with mental patients is gained through a series of part time placements in clinical settings culminating in a one year full time internship. Most clinical psychologists, after graduating, work in settings where their time is distributed between psychodiagnostic work (administering and interpreting tests) and psychotherapy. A significant number also work in academic settings where their time is primarily devoted to teaching and research.

The *psychiatrist*, in contrast, is an M.D. who has spent four years in medical school and completed a three-year psychiatric residency in a clinical setting. During his residency, similar in many ways to an extended internship, he develops clinical skills under the tutelage of more experienced people. Most psychiatrists, after completing their training, spend the greater part of their time conducting therapy in either clinical settings or private practice. Some who work in institutional settings also fill administrative posts. One of the major differences between psychologists and psychiatrists is that the latter, as M.D.s, can prescribe drugs. Their clinical functioning in most other regards is highly similar.

*Psychiatric social workers* attend professional schools of social work and follow a curriculum that focuses on work with the mentally ill. Social work training usually involves two years of full time graduate work and results in a Masters of Social Work (M.S.W.) degree. A significant portion of this time is spent in supervised field work placements in which the student accumulates clinical experience. Psychiatric social workers, after graduating, take positions in a variety of mental health agencies such as hospitals and community clinics. Although many work with individual patients, most tend to focus on helping the families of patients and on developing community resources. Psychiatric social workers, more than psychiatrists and psychologists, act as the link between the mental patient and his community.

As this brief survey indicates, the training of mental health professionals takes many years and involves a substantial amount of personal supervision. The number of people who graduate from professional training programs do not meet the nation's mental health needs. Even if training programs admitted more applicants and were accelerated, the need would still exceed the demand. Taking this into account, the Commission recommended the training of *mental health counselors,* community based workers who would provide direct services for the mentally ill.

The concept of using mental health counselors to treat disturbed individuals rests on the assumption that much of what we call psychopathology actually represents maladaptive ways of dealing with troublesome situations. Deviant behavior, according to this view, is more a function of the ways people react to situational stress than a consequence of long-standing psychological conflict. Under such circumstances, people do not always need, nor can they always afford, a psychiatrist or a psychologist. Charlie Brown's resourceful companion, Snoopy, obviously sympathizes with this view.

In the period since the publication of the Joint Commission's report, a number of mental health counselor training programs have been initiated. In one of the earliest projects, Margaret Rioch (1967) set out to teach inexperienced housewives to do the job of experienced psychotherapists. Recognizing that women comprise one of the largest untapped labor forces in the United States, Rioch selected mature housewives as subjects for her training program. She reasoned that such women might be prime candidates for psychotherapeutic roles because they had accumulated a wealth of interpersonal experience in the course of raising their own families. Rioch writes, "If they have had their eyes open at all, they have had the equivalent of several courses in child development, to say nothing of family dynamics and the problems of adolescence" (1967, p. 111).

Under the auspices of the National Institute of Mental Health, a select group of these housewives were chosen to undergo a two-year training program. During this period, they observed individual and family therapy sessions, attended case seminars, and conducted psychotherapy under the supervision of trained professionals. After completing their training, all of the participants in the project went to work in local community mental health centers.

A follow-up study conducted four years later indicated that all of the

FIGURE 16.

students were still employed. Working as psychotherapists with troubled adolescents and adults, they were regarded favorably by their employers and co-workers. Rioch's pilot project therefore demonstrated that mental health counselors could be trained in relatively short periods of time and could command significant professional respect.

One need not conclude on the basis of Rioch's project, however, that all mental health counselors require intensive training in order to function effectively. In a somewhat different project, untrained college students from Harvard and Brandeis produced significant results working with highly disturbed back ward schizophrenics who were considered unrecoverable. The program consisted of two major elements. One involved students working in groups to improve ward recreational programs. The other required students to work with individual patients in a one-to-one counseling relationship. The program's goal was to improve the social skills of the patients by engaging them in close interpersonal relationships and rekindling their interest in the environment.

Initially the students were not well received. The patients were suspicious and reserved, and ward attendants resented inexperienced individuals pre-empting their roles. This added to the students' own hidden fears and seemed to pose insurmountable barriers. The students nevertheless worked hard to overcome these obstacles and were ultimately able to point to encouraging results. Not only did a number of patients improve, but some were even able to leave the hospital. The statement of one female patient, discharged after spending five years on a chronic ward, reflects the program's impact. Addressing herself to one of the student volunteers, she remarked, "What you did for me was to treat me like a human being, like someone you wanted for a friend and could like" (*Action for Mental Health*, 1961, p. 92–93).

Projects similar to this have been duplicated in other settings (Holzberg *et al.*, 1967) with comparable results and suggest that a potential source of relief for the mental health manpower shortage may lie with the college population. We must consider not only students who will ultimately choose careers in mental health after graduation, but those who could work as part-time mental health counselors while still in school. Sixteen thousand bachelor degrees in psychology were awarded in 1967, and it is estimated that a quarter of a million more will be granted by 1976. Furthermore, there are close to seven million students enrolled in institutions of higher learning. A small number of these students, with only a moderate degree of preparation, could fill a significant part of society's need for manpower to work with the institutionalized mentally ill.

The community mental health movement, in sum, seems to hold promise for the future. But although innovative programs are being developed, conditions do not change overnight; large state institutions still exist and patients still languish in back wards. A large segment of the population still regards the mentally ill with fear and suspicion. However, it is anticipated that some of the developments we have described will eventually eliminate many of these practices as well as the attitudes that underly them.

# Psychotherapy

## chapter five

The treatment of pathological behavior is a complex undertaking that can be approached in many different ways. Some techniques involve biological means, several of which were described in the last chapter. Psychosurgery, shock treatment, and chemotherapy are based on the belief that physical or biochemical changes in the body can produce lasting changes in the patient's behavior. Psychological procedures, in contrast, rest on the assumption that meaningful change can best be promoted through learning, and these methods of treatment are referred to as psychotherapy.

The term "psychotherapy," although widely used, is one of the most misunderstood words in the English language. This is partly due to the fact that there is no one psychotherapeutic process, but many psychotherapies, often with more differences among them than similarities. Confusion also arises from the fact that the meaning of psychotherapy is constantly changing. In the past, the term was only used to denote fairly long-term interactions involving a disturbed person and a highly trained professional. Today it is applied to a variety of interactions (long term and short term, professional and nonprofessional) in which solace, advice, and other forms of help play a central role.

In this chapter we survey some of the major forms of psychotherapy, examining the changes that are taking place within the field. Wherever possible we will show how different methods of treatment are related to different concepts of psychopathology. The various systems are discussed first in terms of individual, and then in terms of group (including community) approaches to treatment.

## Individual Approaches

Individual psychotherapy involves a unique alliance between a troubled individual and a professional specializing in abnormal behavior and human relations. Its uniqueness lies in the functional character of the relationship between the therapist and his client. Unlike other professional affiliations, such as lawyer-client, physician-patient, and so on, psychotherapy uses the relationship *itself* as the primary medium of change.

Since human relationships are highly complex and variable, some psychotherapies last for years while others accomplish what they set out to do in months, even weeks. The duration of therapy is in large part related to the severity of the disturbance as well as to the goals of treatment. Frequently these goals merely center about symptom removal or the reduction of anxiety. However, they may also involve total reorganization of the personality, in which case psychotherapy becomes a much more ambitious undertaking. Irrespective of the particular therapeutic goal, most psychotherapies ultimately aim at some type of meaningful *behavior change*. The patient's ability to modify his distorted beliefs or to better understand his conflicts means little if he is unable to change his behavior so that his existence becomes less painful and more fulfilling.

Among the many different systems of individual psychotherapy[1] are a number of approaches that attempt to alter behavior by first helping the patient view himself and the world in a new light. In these systems, the emphasis is on personality change, with the patient-therapist relationship and insight playing an important role in the change process. A second group stresses symptom removal or the alteration of other concrete behaviors. In these approaches, the patient's view of himself as well as his relationship with the therapist recedes into the background and the emphasis is placed upon the modification of maladaptive habits. The first group of therapies is represented in this chapter by psychoanalysis, the second group by behavior therapy.

### PSYCHOANALYSIS

The psychoanalytic approach to treatment has its origins in the efforts of Freud and Breuer to treat hysteria with hypnosis. Concentrating on neurotics, they proposed that symptoms were associated with early trau-

---

[1] A book entitled *Psychoanalysis and Psychotherapy* (Harper, 1959) lists thirty-six different systems, two-thirds of which are individual therapy.

matic memories that were now unconscious but nevertheless remained influential in the patient's life. According to Freud and Breuer, certain painful experiences in childhood had been pushed into the unconscious through a complex mental operation called *repression*. Lurking as hidden memories in the deepest recesses of the mind, they nevertheless made themselves symbolically known through symptoms. Treatment, for the most part, consisted of using hypnosis to unearth the unconscious memories, enabling the patient to fully experience the intense emotion associated with the original trauma. This process, called *catharsis*, represented the first systematic attempt to treat symptoms by psychological means and ushered in the era of psychotherapy.

The collaboration of Freud and Breuer, although initially successful, soon developed serious strains. One area of disagreement concerned the nature of the patient's repressions. Freud insisted that the patient's unconscious memories stemmed largely from early sexual experiences, an interpretation to which Breuer took strong exception. Another area of conflict centered about the use of hypnosis. Freud found that not all patients could be placed in a deep trance and therefore wanted to abandon the technique. As a result of these and other differences, Freud and Breuer dissolved their professional partnership.

In the years that followed, a number of changes took place in Freud's theory and practice of psychoanalytic therapy. Hypnosis, for one, was used much less frequently and eventually discarded in favor of *free association*, a technique requiring the patient to report anything that passed through his mind no matter how illogical it might seem. Instructed to lie on a couch in a relaxed position, with the therapist out of his field of vision, the patient was told to report past reminiscences, dreams, and even word fragments irrespective of whether they seemed trivial or embarrassing. The fundamental rule of therapy required the patient to be absolutely candid with his therapist. The material generated by this method was felt to be equivalent to the type of material uncovered by hypnosis, although it might emerge more slowly.

In addition to turning from hypnosis to free association, Freud's attention shifted from past traumas to certain unusual developments that seemed to occur regularly in the patient–therapist relationship. He noted in the course of treatment that a great many patients appeared to lose interest in their illness and developed a personal interest in the therapist. This development turned out to be more than just a peculiarity of individual patients and Freud concluded that it held the key to therapeutic change. Labeling it the *transference neurosis*, Freud came to view psychoanalytic treatment in large part as synonymous with the development and resolution of this unique "illness."

The transference neurosis includes spontaneous aggressive and/or erotic responses that arise during the course of treatment and represent the patient's personalization of the therapy. At a certain phase in the therapy process, the patient begins to develop very strong feelings towards the therapist and assumes that the therapist feels similarly. A close examination of the therapist's behavior, however, reveals that the patient's assumptions have no basis in reality; they are simply inappropriate.

These unusual developments can best be understood if we recall that psychoanalytic theory depicts human behavior largely in terms of the cyclic build-up and release of tension associated with impulse expression. For reasons outlined in Chapter 1, the energy discharge associated with the expression of sexual and aggressive impulses can sometimes be blocked, often resulting in the development of neurotic symptoms. These symptoms represent the patient's attempt to discharge the energy associated with the impulse and at the same time disguise its source.

In the same way that energy can be tied to a part of the body (as with a hysterical symptom), or invested in an external object (as in the case of a phobia), it can also be invested in another person; in psychoanalytic treatment, that person is the analyst. During treatment, the energy that was manifested in the neurotic symptom is transferred to the analyst; hence the term "transference neurosis" to describe the patient's inappropriate behavior during the course of treatment. The *intrapsychic* disturbance has been transformed into an *interpersonal* one, producing an artificial illness that can be dealt with more efficiently in therapy. The transference neurosis now represents the patient's attempt to gratify his impulses, and affords the therapist an opportunity to observe directly how the patient dealt with early frustrations.

Since the patient's frustrations occurred early in life, in the context of intense parent–child interactions, we find, not too surprisingly, that the patient unconsciously places the analyst in the role of parental figure. The result is a replay of an archaic but nevertheless powerful drama in which the therapist is symbolically recast as a authoritative parent. An example of the transference neurosis is seen in the following excerpt taken from a psychoanalytic session. In this session, the patient, a woman with strong homosexual tendencies, relates a fantasy regarding a vague figure with whom she would like to sleep. Some of the therapist's unspoken reflections are contained in brackets.

PT: And then I come to think about what would this man have to look like. From his shoulders, right around about here—and that's you. It just came to me. The man is you. I have been thinking these thoughts since I started coming here, sex thoughts.

TH: The man is I?

PT: Yeah.

TH: Mm hmm.

PT:   I got, I got those feelings of sex now that are driving me crazy. By god, I didn't know I could ever say that.

TH:   You couldn't say that to me?

PT:   No, no. Well, but I did. But I thought, "Well, maybe it's not so. Maybe it's just nonsense." But the more I thought about it, the more it was you. I tried to push it out of my mind, but it's true.

TH:   Maybe that's why you were upset.

PT:   It's possibly that. But it's a horrible thought that I can think that. I remember seeing daddy without his clothes. His penis seemed enormous. I get a funny feeling. It's repulsive and exciting too. Just like I feel about you. I try not to think about it. [It is apparent that her feelings toward me are projections of her feelings toward her father.]

TH:   What about your sex feelings about men?

PT:   Zero. That's why it's so funny I feel this way about you. It makes me upset to think about it. [The need to repress incestuous impulses probably inhibits her sexual feelings toward all men.]

TH:   Perhaps you feel it's wrong to feel sex about men.

PT:   I just have no feeling about it. Maybe it's safer that way.

TH:   Maybe it's safer to feel sexy toward women, because it's not safe to feel sexy with men? [interpreting her homosexuality]

PT:   Definitely. (Wolberg, 1954, p. 408–9)

We can see the patient attempt first to deal with her strong sexual impulses by unconsciously thrusting them upon the analyst. Her associations, however, lead her to consider a similar childhood reaction to her father, a reaction whose significance was repressed. The analyst follows up on this by interpreting her revulsion to men as a derivative of her incestuous wish.

The resolution of the transference neurosis sees the patient come to grips with whatever unrealistic expectations have developed in the course of treatment. Through repeated interpretations, the therapist shows the patient how transference behaviors represent nothing more than phantom responses whose origins lie in the forgotten past. The patient's eventual appreciation of this is what is meant by the term *insight*.

Successful completion of therapy, however, requires the patient not only to recognize the complex interconnections between his childhood conflicts and his behavior in therapy, but to understand how this relates to his current adult relationships. He must be able to appreciate how his current sexual problems with his wife, for example, are intimately related to similar sexual feelings held for his mother, feelings that have been repressed for years; he must learn that his current anxiety attacks in the presence of authority figures stem from repressed feelings toward his father. This process, referred to as *working through*, sometimes takes years to complete. However, once it is completed, the patient is supposedly better able to realistically deal with his impulses, successfully gratify his interpersonal needs, and lead a more productive life.

The term "psychoanalysis" often is mistakenly confused with the term "psychotherapy." Psychoanalysis, however, is only one form of psycho-therapy, and a highly specialized one at that. Standard psychoanalytic treatment requires four to five sessions per week and lasts from two to five years. It is a very time consuming and expensive process and thus can be utilized only by a very limited segment of the population. In addition, only a very small proportion of all practicing therapists are psychoanalysts. Most current psychotherapy based on Freudian principles, consequently, falls into the category of *analytic therapy*.

*Analytic therapy* differs from classical psychoanalysis in several im-portant respects, perhaps the most important of which concerns the fate of the transference neurosis. In analytic therapy, the development of the transference neurosis is discouraged and virtually eliminated as the medium of therapeutic change. The dependency of the patient on his analyst, which in psychoanalysis underlies the development of the transference neurosis, is minimized in analytic therapy by reducing contacts from five times a week to once or twice a week, and by dispensing with the couch and free association in favor of face to face discussion. The therapist in analytic therapy, moreover, is relatively more active and verbal. This is in contrast to classical psychoanalysis where the therapist deliberately remains vague and noncommittal to provide the "blank screen" upon which the patient can project his infantile fantasies.

Unlike psychoanalysis, which has as its focus the resolution of childhood conflicts as they arise in the transference neurosis, analytic therapy focuses upon concrete difficulties that currently disrupt the patient's life on anal-ysis of current problems rather than on analysis of the therapeutic relation-ship. In analytic treatment, greater time is spent, for example, studying alternative ways that the patient might deal with his spouse or employer, than in delving into the past. Analytic therapy, consequently, is usually briefer, more problem oriented, and less of an intrapsychic ordeal.

Although psychoanalysis and its variants differ in their approach to treatment, both rely on a cooperative, somewhat verbal, patient who is willing to embark on a collaborative and often stressful venture for future benefits that are only dimly perceived. For these reasons, psychoanalytic techniques are rather unsuited for work with psychotic patients, particularly schizophrenics. The ability to commit oneself to an extended relationship and the motivation needed to undergo the slow and painful process of self-exploration is usually lacking in schizophrenic patients. Other tech-niques, one of which we consider next, seem better able to cope with patients who are difficult to deal with in conventional ways.

DIRECTIVE THERAPY

This approach to treatment takes as its point of departure the patient–therapist relationship and focuses on the ways participants try to manipulate each other. The theoretical underpinnings of directive therapy are contained in human communication theory and were introduced in Chapter 3 under the heading of the double bind. To review briefly, all interactions between human beings are construed in terms of the messages transmitted between the individuals involved. Because of the complexities of communicational processes, multiple messages may be transmitted simultaneously and in some instances can convey conflicting information. When this occurs, and one of the participants (the victim) is so highly dependent upon the other that he cannot leave the field, a double bind is said to exist. Whatever move the victim makes, he loses; he is damned if he does and damned if he doesn't.

Extending these concepts more generally, communication theorists propose that all interpersonal messages act to define the characteristics of a relationship. Communications dictate *what* is to take place in a relationship and who is in control. To use a simple example, the student who addresses Professor Charles Smith as "Charlie" structures their relationship as one between friends or equals. Neither of the members can be said to be in control, assuming that both are comfortable on a first name basis. If, however, "Charlie" insists that he be addressed as Professor Smith, he has taken it upon himself to structure their interaction hierarchically, as one of teacher and student, and thus has assumed control of the relationship.[2]

According to Jay Haley (1963), one of the originators of double-bind theory, trying to gain control of a relationship is not pathological—to do so while denying it, is. A symptom is a way of controlling a relationship while simultaneously denying it; it is a tactic in human relations. The housewife whose constant dizzy spells force her husband to do the housework, controls his behavior while denying it ("I can't help being dizzy"). The hysterical patient who forces others to minister to his needs or who solicits endless attention, also controls those about him. He too "cannot help" being sick. In both instances, the symptom functions as a double-binding communication. It signals "I am helpless" while simultaneously circumscribing the behavior of others.

Since the patient's illness within this approach is viewed in terms of deviant communication patterns, the ultimate goal of treatment is to help him communicate more directly with others. The immediate goal of therapy, however, is to get the patient to give up his symptom so that he might communicate in a more direct fashion with the therapist. Achieving this entails construction of therapeutic double binds that place the patient in an untenable position from which he cannot escape unless he relinquishes his symptom. This is accomplished through the use of *paradoxical injunc-*

[2] The student, of course, could continue to address Professor Smith by his first name thus making him very uncomfortable. In that case, the student is in control since he retains the upper hand.

*tions*—double-binding commands that encourage the symptom in such a way that the patient cannot continue to use it.

Perhaps the simplest example of a paradoxical injunction is the command "Be spontaneous!" The only way one can follow this command is *not* to follow it. In directive psychotherapy, paradoxical injunctions take the form of prescribing the symptom. The therapist treats the symptom by directing the patient to engage in symptomatic behavior! A clinical example of this technique is described in the case of a college student who was in danger of failing her courses because of an inability to get up for eight o'clock classes before ten o'clock. A therapist using directive techniques agreed to try to help her if she would explicitly follow his directions, an agreement to which she readily agreed.

> She was then told to set her alarm clock for seven o'clock. The following morning, when the alarm went off, she would find herself faced with two alternatives: she could either get up, have breakfast, and be in class by eight, in which case nothing further was to be done about the whole matter; or she could stay in bed, as usual. In the latter case, however, she would not be allowed to get up shortly before ten, as she used to, but she would have to reset the alarm to *eleven* A.M. and stay in bed on this and on the following morning until it went off. For these two mornings, she would not be allowed to read, write, listen to the radio or do anything else except to sleep or just lie in bed; after eleven she could do whatever she wanted. On the evening of the second day she was to set the alarm again for seven A.M., and if she was again unable to get up when it rang, she would again have to stay in bed until eleven on that and the following morning, and so on. Finally, he completed the double bind by telling her that if she did not live up to the terms of this agreement, which she had accepted of her own free will, he would no longer be of any use to her as her therapist and would, therefore, have to discontinue the treatment. The girl was delighted with this apparently pleasant instruction. When she came back for her next session three days later, she reported that she had as usual been unable to get up in time the first morning, that she had stayed in bed until after eleven as instructed, but that this enforced bed rest (and especially the time from ten to eleven) had been almost unbearably boring. The second morning had been even worse, and she was totally unable to sleep a minute longer than seven even though the alarm did not, of course, go off until eleven. From then on she attended her morning classes, and only then was it possible to enter into an exploration of the reasons that seemingly made it compulsory for her to fail in college. (Watzlawick *et al.*, 1967, p. 249)

In this example, we see the therapeutic use of a double bind to counteract the communicational double bind that the patient employs, her symptom. If she complies with the therapist's directions, she no longer can claim that staying in bed is outside of her control. If she resists his command, she can only do so by *not* behaving symptomatically. No matter what she does, she loses. But by losing, she wins.

The premise underlying the treatment of the student in the preceding case study remains essentially the same in work with schizophrenics. The schizophrenic's psychotic symptomatology (bizarre use of language, social withdrawal, and delusional beliefs) are construed within this approach as the patient's attempt to radically curtail involvement with other human beings. Every one of his symptoms functions to effectively communicate that what he does is not a response to social stimuli. Psychotherapy, accordingly, is designed to force the schizophrenic to relate to the therapist using whatever techniques seem appropriate. In Haley's words, "it is necessary to persuade or force the patient to respond in such a way that he is consistently indicating what kind of relationship he has with the therapist instead of indicating that what he does is not in response to the therapist" (1963, p. 102).

One way of accomplishing this is to prescribe or encourage the schizophrenic's behavior in much the same way that the student's staying in bed was prescribed. This technique was employed in the case of a patient who harbored a persecutory delusion, a delusion that lead him to suspect that someone had planted a hidden microphone in the therapist's office.

> Rather than trying to interpret this suspicion, the therapist became "appropriately" concerned and put the patient into a therapeutic double bind by suggesting that together they make a thorough search of the office before proceeding with the session. This left the patient with an illusion of alternatives: he could accept the search or dismiss the paranoid idea. He chose the former alternative, and as the search painstakingly got under way, he became increasingly unsure and embarrassed about his suspicion; but the therapist would not let the matter rest until every nook and cranny of the office had been explored by them together. (Watzlawick, 1967, p. 243)

The patient ultimately relinquished his symptom and began to engage in meaningful discussion with the therapist. Had he initially refused to take the therapist's suggestion to search the office, he would have labeled his suspicion as foolish or inconsequential. In either case, the paradoxical prescription achieved its aims.

There are many cases of schizophrenia in which the patient is so withdrawn or uncooperative that it is impossible to get him to make even minimal social responses. In cases of this sort, the therapist may have to resort to force in order to get the patient to interact. This is vividly portrayed in excerpts from an account of a therapy session involving a therapist, his assistants, and a schizophrenic patient who claimed he was God.

PT:   I am God. (Laughter in background)
TH:   You!

PT: Yes.

TH: You crazy dope (laughs). Kneel in front of me!

PT: No, you kneel in front of me.

TH: Boys, show him who's God. (The assistants struggle with the patient, forcing him to his knees in front of the therapist.)

PT: Now listen . . .

TH: Kneel in front of me!

PT: You're not supposed to use force against me.

TH: Don't be silly, I'm the boss.

ASST: Now he's on his knees.

TH: Now—what are you doing? . . .

PT: Look, you're not supposed to use force against me.

TH: I'm boss here.

PT: You're not supposed to use force—you're not boss here.

TH: Who's God?

PT: I am God.

TH: Well, why don't you get up then?

PT: Well, I'll push them away—tell them to get away.

TH: All right boys, get away.

PT: That was a mistake, I should have pushed them then. (The patient laughs and everyone laughs.) I should have obliterated them.

ASST: (Laughing) Obliterate, yeah.

TH: Obliterate, that's it. (pause) You're absolutely helpless. [The interview continues.] (Haley, 1963, pp. 99–100)

Here again, the issue that arises between patient and therapist is: who is going to dictate what goes on in the relationship? In this case the patient attempts to control the interaction by claiming he is God, in effect declaring that he need not relate to anything the therapist says or does. The therapist double-binds him by forcing him to his knees. If the patient continues to insist he is God, he finds himself in the untenable position of having to concede that God is subservient to the therapist. If he stops insisting that he is God, he finds himself relating to the therapist in a manner that is decidedly nonschizophrenic. Within this singular approach, schizophrenia is not viewed as a disease entity; there is no such thing as "a schizophrenic," only schizophrenic ways of relating.

The directive approach to treatment occupies a unique theoretical position in that it constitutes an interesting blend of the intrapsychic and behavioristic models. The approach approximates behavior therapy in that it tends to focus on the patient's symptoms and the ways they might be eliminated. Unlike behavior therapy, however, the directive approach tends to regard this only as a preliminary treatment tactic: eliminating symptomatic behavior simply opens avenues to more fruitful discussions of the patient's interpersonal difficulties. In this regard, the approach is similar to the intrapsychic model where symptoms merely represent more serious and pervasive pathology. In the next section we examine those therapies in which symptom removal becomes the only goal of treatment.

BEHAVIOR THERAPY

Behavior therapy, or behavior modification, approaches disordered behavior from the view of experimental learning theory. Within this framework, symptoms as well as other forms of maladaptive behavior are learned and, like any other behavior, can be unlearned. Stated succinctly, the symptom is the illness. Learning concepts, accordingly, can be applied to an understanding of abnormal behavior without recourse to formulations involving personality constructs and hidden conflicts. Derived from the behavioristic model of abnormal behavior, behavior therapy has grown to the point where it offers a powerful alternative to the intrapsychic modes of treatment.

Much of the impetus behind the growth of behavioral techniques in the past two decades can be traced to a growing disenchantment with the intrapsychic approaches, particularly psychoanalysis. Even under the best conditions, most analytically based approaches are expensive and time consuming. Even when effective, they depend on the active participation of a highly verbal, intellectually-oriented patient, usually someone from the middle or upper-middle class. Recalling the inverse relationship between mental illness and social class discussed in Chapter 3, it is apparent that the intrapsychic therapies are unable to provide the answers to the nation's therapeutic needs except on a limited scale. Behavior therapy, with its claims of quick effective relief and its pragmatic focus on troublesome behavior, seems to be a viable alternative to many psychologists.

There are many different forms of behavior therapy, all of which focus on the elimination of symptoms, broadly construed as any form of observable, maladaptive behavior. Most of these therapies have their ideological roots either in the early work of Pavlov and Watson or in the more recent formulations of B.F. Skinner. The former group, with its emphasis on classical conditioning, is represented in this chapter by a technique called systematic desensitization. The latter group, emphasizing the use of operant techniques, is depicted by recent attempts to treat a serious childhood disorder called autism.

*Systematic desensitization*, a form of psychotherapy developed by a psychiatrist named Joseph Wolpe, is mostly used to treat phobias. The theory underlying this method is rather straightforward and was presented in Chapter 1. Reviewing briefly, phobias are construed as anxiety *responses* (rapid breathing, tense musculature, cold sweats, and so on) that are elicited by relatively harmless phobic *stimuli* (closed spaces, heights, snakes). These stimuli and responses have, over a period of time, become regularly associated so that strong *S–R* (stimulus–response) *bonds* exist. Whenever these stimuli are encountered, the phobic response, anxiety, automatically occurs. The therapeutic task is to weaken and ultimately break these S–R bonds.

Systematic desensitization is a method designed to weaken such bonds by gradually replacing anxiety with other, more adaptive, responses. The technique gently leads the patient through a series of graded anxiety experiences (situations similar to the original phobic situation but less frightening) and *systematically* substitutes new behaviors for anxiety.[3] In this way, the patient is progressively *desensitized* to the original phobic situation and thus cured of his neurosis. Hence, the term systematic desensitization.

To facilitate this process, the therapist employs two basic devices, relaxation training and an anxiety hierarchy. *Relaxation training* involves teaching the patient to breathe more smoothly, relax his limbs, and slacken his facial muscles. He must be able to execute these responses on cue, for the entire therapeutic procedure depends upon his ability to effectively substitute relaxation for anxiety responses at the right moment.

The *anxiety hierarchy* is a list of objects or situations resembling, in varying degrees, the phobic situation. These are ordered in such a way as to make each successive step on the hierarchy more anxiety inducing than the one that precedes it. A typical anxiety hierarchy for a patient who has a snake phobia might be:

1. Reading a magazine article about snakes
2. Looking at photographs of snakes
3. Standing outside a reptile house at the zoo
4. Standing near a snake cage inside the reptile house
5. Placing hand in cage without touching snakes
6. Touching snakes.

Hierarchies such as this, graded from mild to high levels of anxiety, are constructed from information the patient provides regarding his most frightening experience and situations related to it.

The therapeutic procedure involves several steps. First, the therapist trains the patient in the relaxation procedures so that relaxation responses can be produced on cue. This usually takes four to six sessions. The patient is then asked to vividly imagine the scene depicted on the first step of the hierarchy. If he becomes tense and apprehensive, he is immediately told to call forth the relaxation responses he was taught earlier. Since it is impossible to be anxious and relaxed at the same time, the stimulus' ability to evoke anxiety is weakened. After repeated trials of this sort, with a concomitant reduction in anxiety, the patient is able to move on to the next level.

---

[3] Although a variety of novel behaviors can be used as substitutes, relaxation responses often are chosen because they are relatively easy to learn.

This procedure is systematically repeated until the patient masters the highest step on the hierarchy, in our example, touching a snake. When he can vividly imagine doing this, without getting excessively anxious, therapy is terminated. It is assumed, of course, that his newly acquired responses will generalize and that he will be able to confront the phobic stimulus in reality with relative calm. Systematic desensitization, in sum, replaces one conditioned response (anxiety) with another (relaxation) and, as a result, eliminates the patient's phobia.

In the operant approach to treatment, the focus shifts from concentration on S–R bonds to the *consequences* of the patient's behavior. Of particular interest is the way certain reinforcements (rewards and punishment) control the patient's actions and lead him to behave in deviant ways. By analyzing the relationship between deviant behavior and its consequences, the behavior therapist seeks to modify the latter, thereby bringing the behavior in question under control. An example of this process is seen in the efforts of O. Ivar Lovaas and his associates to treat early childhood autism.

*Early childhood autism* is a schizophrenic-like disturbance characterized by atypical behavior, disturbance in speech, and an inability to relate to other human beings. The autistic child's unusual behavior is often noted early in life and includes strange physical movements and distorted facial expressions. In some cases, brutal and indiscriminant self-mutilation is also seen. Autistic children have been known to remove large sections of flesh from their bodies with their teeth and to break their noses by striking their heads against solid objects.

Lack of speech development and rejection of others nevertheless constitute the most common features of the autistic syndrome. Many autistic children are mute, and those who do speak either are *echolalic* (repeat back only what is said to them) or merely emit vowel sounds. Children of this sort are virtually oblivious to their social surroundings and normal social reinforcements such as affection, support, and attention simply have no impact on them.

In the years since autism was first documented, there have been attempts to treat these children by a variety of different methods. Individual psychotherapy, with its attempt to build a close relationship with the child, has been used most often, although play therapy in groups has also been tried. Although isolated successes have been reported, the overall picture is generally disappointing. Most autistic children show little if any improvement even after years of intensive treatment. Many end up spending the rest of their lives confined in institutions.

More recently, O. Ivar Lovaas and his associates at the UCLA School of Medicine have experimented with a variety of behavioristic techniques designed to reduce mutilation, encourage development of speech, and promote the growth of human relationships. One of his studies involved the use of negative reinforcement as a means of building social behavior (Lovaas *et al.*, 1965). In negative reinforcement, the patient is exposed to an unpleasant, usually painful, stimulus that is removed as soon as he emits the behavior the experimenter is seeking. The behavior sought in this case was movement towards adult figures and the negative reinforcer employed was painful shock.

Lovaas' study was carried out on a pair of identical twins, five years of age, both of whom were diagnosed as childhood schizophrenics. The children did not speak, were not toilet trained, and spent most of their days rocking themselves to and fro. They were totally unresponsive to social stimuli, showed no signs of recognizing adults, and even ignored one another. Lovaas points out that although they had been treated intensively in a residential treatment center, there had been no significant change in their behavior, and their future was certain institutionalization.

The experimental procedure separately placed each child in a small room whose floor was gridded with half-inch wide electrical strips. The strips were set a half-inch apart so the child could not avoid stepping on at least two strips; when this happened, the circuit would close, giving the child a strong electrical shock. The general plan was to teach the child what was expected of him and if he did not respond, shock him until he did.

During several pretraining sessions in which no shock was used, each child was placed in the room with two adults who repeatedly invited him to "come here." Neither child responded. In subsequent shock sessions spaced over three consecutive days and involving many, many trials, the children were trained to avoid shock by responding to the adults' verbal command. On each trial, shock was withheld if the child approached the attending adults within five seconds. If he did not make a move in this time, or if he was not within a foot of the experimenters within seven seconds, shock was delivered until he responded.

The results indicated that both children learned to successfully avoid shock by responding to the commands of the attending adults. Whereas before the experiment they were simply unresponsive to any form of social stimulation, afterwards they sought physical contact with the adults and even made efforts to observe them. By rescuing the children, the adults thus were able to take on rewarding properties. The improvement that was recorded also generalized beyond the experimental room. The nurses who cared for the children reported that the two now came to them for help when they were hurt, something that they had not done before the experiment.

Although such findings are encouraging, we must point out that the changes were temporary and lasted only from nine to eleven months. Even had such changes lasted longer, one still would have to contend with the fact that the children remained nonverbal, an extremely negative indication past the age of four or five. If a child is beyond this age and still cannot speak, his chances for recovery are very slim. There are no miracle cures in this area and behavior therapy is not a panacea, something Lovaas is the first to admit. He writes,

> It is a mistake to refer to this therapy as "operant conditioning therapy" since operant conditioning provides for only a beginning. Accordingly, our formulations cannot account for a child's becoming "normal" if this should happen in our setting because they do not describe all the nuances of man's interaction with his environment. There is more to human behavior than that contained within reinforcement theory. (1967, p. 110)

Lovaas' statement helps to temper some of the arguments between proponents of the intrapsychic and behavioristic approaches to treatment. One of these revolves about the issue of "symptom substitution." The behaviorists, as we have seen, regard symptoms simply as maladaptive behavior that needs to be eliminated or replaced. The intrapsychic therapists, particularly those who adopt the psychoanalytic view, see symptoms as reflections of a more serious disturbance. In much the same way that physicians view fever as a reflection of an underlying infection, the analytic therapist views symptoms as an indication of a more basic underlying disorder. Treat the fever and you still have not dealt with the infection; treat the symptom and you still have not dealt with the psychopathology.

According to psychoanalytic theory, treatment that is merely symptomatic leads only to temporary relief. The disorder will simply make itself known in the guise of another symptom and the patient will be just as sick as before he began treatment. Behavioristic clinicians contend that this does not happen and claim recovery rates of up to ninety percent with few relapses. Yet, patients have been relieved of a symptom only to become depressed later. Is depression a symptom? Is occasional sadness? What happens in cases where symptoms are eradicated and then prove to have been only part of a more serious picture? Perhaps, there are some disorders in which symptoms are only symbolic indications of inner distress and others in which they constitute the entire disturbance.

Recalling what Lovaas had to say, we might conjecture that certain forms of psychopathology, whatever their origins, may be handled more profitably by means of behavioristic techniques than others. Disturbances that present themselves in observable, concrete ways, for example, may be handled best by one of the behavior therapies. Phobias, enuresis (chronic bed wetting), and other forms of relatively circumscribed disorders would probably fall in this category. Disturbances involving depression, social inferiority, and interpersonal alienation, on the other hand, may require approaches that focus on the subtleties of human relationships. In such instances, certain intrapsychic approaches or group therapies, to which we turn next, may prove to be more appropriate.

## Group and Community Approaches

Although individual psychotherapy predates group therapy, the idea of using groups to treat disturbed individuals is not particularly new. Psychotherapists have conducted group therapy for over thirty years, and Jacob Moreno, the founder of a method called Psychodrama, claims to have used group techniques as far back as 1910. In recent times, however, there has been a remarkable upsurge in the popularity of the group approach. Part of the reason may be the tremendous publicity therapy groups receive in the media; another is the search for intimacy and relatedness among the growing number of people who feel increasingly alienated from society. Whatever the reason, traditional psychotherapy groups, as well as family groups and community treatment methods, seem to be addressing themselves to issues that individual therapy cannot. In the remainder of the chapter, we consider what these issues are and the ways groups attempt to deal with them.

### GROUP PSYCHOTHERAPY

Group therapy involves a gathering of approximately six to eight persons who usually meet once or twice a week for about an hour and a half. The group, usually made up of strangers, meets regularly for six months to a year, although these figures vary depending on the makeup of the group and the goals it sets for itself. Most groups tend to be relatively homogeneous with regard to the types of disturbance presented by its members. We thus find addict groups (Alcoholics Anonymous and Synanon) and groups composed solely of neurotics or psychotics. Under circumstances where people are expected to share their problems, common experiences tend to facilitate individual expression.

The direction a group takes depends, in large part, on the orientation of its therapist. Analytically oriented therapists tend to steer their groups toward discussion of the past and toward consideration of hidden fantasies. The relationships of the members towards one another are examined for indications of transference in much the same way that transference attitudes towards the analyst are examined in individual treatment. The client-centered therapist, in contrast, tries to foster a group atmosphere in which members communicate empathy and acceptance for one another. The members receive from each other what they would have received from their therapist had they been engaged in individual client-centered therapy.

But group therapy involves more than just a translation of individual techniques into group terms. It involves concentration on the group as an entity in its own right. The focus in many groups thus shifts from the personality characteristics of the group members to the dynamics of their interaction. These dynamics are then analyzed to ascertain which types of behavior promote or inhibit the group's ability to function as an effective problem solving unit. Within this perspective, issues of interpersonal attraction, group cohesiveness, and group development emerge as subjects for consideration. As the group becomes a more effective interactional unit, it is assumed that important personal learning takes place, learning that generalizes to more effective functioning outside the group.

Within the group approach to treatment, the therapist is not viewed as the primary agent of change; it is the patients themselves who fulfill this role. By honestly voicing their immediate reactions to one another, the various group members help each other test the validity of their self-perceptions. Every member is thus provided the opportunity to change his behavior in light of the feedback he receives. By encouraging such change, the group functions as a multipronged agent of change with each participant acting as therapist for the other. The actual therapist, while less active than he would be in individual therapy, still plays a significant role; adopting the position of a participant observer, he guides the group's overall movement and intervenes primarily at times when the group process falters.

Describing group therapy via written excerpts is a formidable task. Not only does the psychotherapeutic process continue over a long period of time, but it is especially difficult to capture the essence of multiple relationships in a few words. Nevertheless the following excerpt provides a beginning glimpse of what this process involves. In this passage, a group member who has difficulties in his relationships with women begins by noting a recent dream regarding the group. The therapist's private thoughts are enclosed in brackets.

DAN: Gee, I had a dream last night about this group. I dreamt that we were in the group. I was sitting there. Joe was sitting here and Joe was talking about something—I don't know what he was talking about. I seen a bunch of people start looking through the window. Loads of people, I told you, and you called the police and you made a big speech about twenty minutes about privacy.

THERAPIST: You had it last night?

DAN: Yeah, nothing happened—I came home about ten o'clock last night, had some dinner and went to bed. Lots of tension between my father and I. As we get busy, the tension grows, and we kill each other. And I got nothing against him and suppose he got nothing against me, but we just let it out to each other. Terrible wrangling and fighting.

THERAPIST: What do you feel about the dream?

DAN: Somebody's spying on me, or the group is going to see me for what I am or something like that. They were actually looking in.

MARLENE: You were saying last week that you spoke very freely on the outside. It's only in the group that you don't speak freely. . . .

FRITZI: What are you afraid that we're going to find out about you that you don't want to expose? [The expression of concern.]

DAN: Nothing.

RON: Maybe you're afraid that the other people will find out that you're going to a group.

DAN: Yeah.

FRITZI: Do you feel your parents spy on you? You know, your mother?

DAN: I can't stand her guts lately. I just don't talk to her. I keep away from her, because every time I look at her I want to yell at her or fight or something. . . .

THERAPIST: What picture of yourself do you have that the group is going to find out? [The "self-concept" is questioned.]

DAN: I don't know. I know the picture I have of myself, but it's something the group knows.

THERAPIST: What's that?

DAN: That I'm shit. The more I go out, the more I complain. There can't be something wrong with so many girls—percentage-wise—proportionate, all right, but not so many girls. I do go out week after week with a different girl. I see a hell of a lot of girls every year.

RON: Fifty-two.

DAN: Sunday nights sometimes, too. Sometimes during the week.

RON: Each time it's a different girl?

DAN: Yeah, used to go out five times a week sometimes. All different.

RON: Yeah, but the next week are there five different more?

DAN: Yeah. Very rarely take a girl out twice.

RON: Why do you think this is so?

DAN: I don't know. It's probably me.

FRITZI: No, if you don't get to know them too well they'll never find out about you, so you can leave them with the big-shot impression if you only see them once. [The interpretation.] (Mullan and Rosenbaum, 1962, pp. 173–75)

Even though this passage covers the span of only a few minutes in a single session, it serves to demonstrate how the various group members, through feedback and interpretation, take on therapeutic roles. The major learning that evolves from a group experience, in sum, thus derives as much from the patient's interaction with his fellow patients as from direct interchanges with the therapist.

## FAMILY GROUP THERAPY

Family therapy differs from most other group approaches to treatment in that the participants already constitute an existing unit. The disturbed family brings with it into treatment patterns of deviance that have a long established history. Despite this, families in need of help rarely see themselves as disturbed or as having family difficulties. More often than not, they arrive at a clinic with a disturbed child and present *him* as their reason for being there.

The major assumption underlying family treatment is that the child's symptoms are a reflection of the family's interpersonal conflicts. It is invariably the family rather than the child that is considered the patient. The child's behavior merely functions as a mask for some of the more serious problems that exist in the family, problems which originally may not have even involved the child. A dominance struggle between the father and mother, for example, may be played out in a conflict over the issue of discipline. The child consequently finds himself playing the part of a helpless pawn in a struggle that is not of his doing. Caught between warring forces, he responds by developing symptoms, failing in school, and behaving in other ways that represent his response to the predicament he finds himself in. We might note in passing that this view of family pathology is simply a social derivative of the intrapsychic model. Symptoms, rather than reflecting an *intrapsychic* conflict, now reflect an *intrafamilial* one.

Two ways in which family pathology is sustained are through scapegoating and through the development of covert alliances. In *scapegoating*, one of the children is subtly blamed for whatever family difficulties may arise. Conversations in scapegoating families often are punctuated with remarks such as, "If Jimmy weren't so sick, we all would be getting along so well." They rarely consider the converse, that Jimmy wouldn't be so sick if they were all getting along better. *Covert alliances* exist when two or more members of a family secretly join to form a close bond at another member's expense. Mothers (or fathers) who feel rejected by their spouse sometimes retaliate by forming overly close bonds with their children and subtly influencing them to exclude the other parent. In this way, they are able to indirectly express the anger they could not communicate directly. Family therapy attempts to change destructive patterns such as these by opening up congested channels of communications, reducing defensiveness, and helping to create an atmosphere of family reciprocity.

John Bell, one of the early workers in the area of family therapy, conceptualizes this form of treatment in terms of a series of stages (1961). After some initial orientation sessions, he sees therapy passing through the following phases:

> Child-centered phase
> Parent-child interaction phase
> Father-mother interaction phase
> Sibling interaction phase
> Family centered phase

The initial stage sees the child placed in the center of the group, and given the opportunity to air his complaints. In the process he is encouraged to suggest the types of changes he would like to see. During the middle stages, the focus is on the different types of familial interactions with the various members encouraged to explore the stereotyped generalizations they hold about one another. A common topic during these stages is the manner in which each member interferes with clear family communication. In the final stage, the entire family discusses the meaning of productive family life and the ways each can provide support for the other in the roles they play.

As in the case with most forms of group therapy, the reality testing provided by interpersonal feedback constitutes an important part of the treatment process. In one case seen by the author, an adolescent boy (the patient) was brought by his parents to a clinic to help him with recurrent feelings of depression (the problem). After a series of diagnostic interviews, it was suggested that the family be seen together in family therapy. During therapy, the father revealed that he spent a great deal of time with his son trying to be a good father and "a buddy." As therapy progressed and the boy felt freer to say what was on his mind, he confronted the father with the fact that he viewed him not as helpful and friendly but as bothersome and controlling. The father initially was shocked and dismayed but realized that he was only working against himself and backed off. Soon thereafter, his relationship with his son improved. Later in therapy it turned out that his overinvestment in his son compensated for marital difficulty that he and his wife were experiencing. Much of the remaining therapy involved working through problems in the marital relationship.

Family therapy is a relatively recent innovation in the area of group therapy and there still is much experimentation. Although most family therapists tend to work exclusively with the nuclear family, parents and children, some work with the extended family. By including grandparents in therapy, the therapist provides the family members with the opportunity to make cross-generational parent-child comparisons. Some therapists even include friends and neighbors. Dr. Ross Speck, a psychiatrist working in the family area, attempts to draw other families and peers of the patient into what he calls "network" therapy (1967). Speck sees the family network, a loosely defined group of friends, relatives, and neighbors, as a potent social system, one capable of creating significant family change. Peers can be used to provide attention and support for a distressed child when parents become embroiled in marital conflicts. Neighbors can be called upon to intervene in the innumerable crises that disturbed families always seem to create. Relatives, finally, can offer temporary refuge for children who are victims of scapegoating. Although it is considered quite radical, network therapy is perhaps no more innovative than family therapy was 10 or 15 years ago when the idea of treating the family as a unit was first proposed.

The two forms of group therapy that have been discussed up to this point share a number of important characteristics. Both emphasize the value of talking out one's problems and both require somewhat of an extended commitment. Until quite recently, most prospective group participants could expect to spend a rather long period of time involved in the slow process of self-exploration. In the past decade, however, there has been a proliferation of new techniques with a corresponding deemphasis on the need for intellectual analyses or extended commitment. The new look involves feeling instead of intellectualization, and short- rather than long-term involvement. For want of a better title, these are discussed under the heading of the "new groups."

### THE NEW GROUPS

Groups falling under this rubric are short-term affairs whose duration is measured in days rather than months, with treatment often beginning and ending over a weekend. Known under such names as Sensitivity, Encounter, Gestalt, and Marathon groups, they offer the subscriber the potential for substantial help in a relatively short period of time.

Although there is an endless variety of these groups, most have their beginnings either in the work of the Esalen Institute in Big Sur, California, or the National Training Laboratories (NTL) in Bethel, Maine. At Esalen, where the Encounter group originated, the emphasis is on promoting change through intense personal interaction and body awareness. Stress is placed upon physical experiences (dance, massage, touch) and the key words are *individual growth*. The National Training Labs also aim at producing change through intense personal interchanges. At NTL, where Sensitivity groups were developed, the focus, however, is on community or *organizational growth*. NTL-trained people are more likely to be called upon to help improve black-white relations in racially tense communities, or to solve personnel problems in industry.

Both Encounter and Sensitivity groups are basically designed to promote healthier relationships by encouraging more open, honest communication. While an admirable goal, this is easier said than done. Human beings, generally speaking, rarely divulge what they really think of each other, nor do they readily reveal personal information of an intimate nature. Most people are careful to hide their true feelings either to maintain appearances or to avoid becoming dangerously vulnerable. The new groups, by encouraging frankness and self-disclosure, attempt to change this.

Most of the activities in these groups revolve about the direct, unbridled expression of emotions. Immediate expression of feelings and self-revelation are valued highly with intellectual reflection and cognitive understanding taking a back seat. Members are forced to reveal what they are really like by letting down their defenses and divesting themselves of their inhibitions. The phrase "letting it all hang out" captures the sometimes brutal self-exposure and open display of feelings that the new groups insist upon. Participants in these groups are asked to step outside their customary social roles, remove their masks (and sometimes their clothes), and be themselves.

The process that facilitates such behavior, comprising a blend of confrontation techniques and nonverbal exercises, forces participants to examine the extent to which they are in touch with their feelings. This is accomplished by getting group members to carefully explore their emotions as they take place in the here-and-now. Members are asked to deal with their feelings as they occur in the room (the "here"), at the moment they occur (the "now"), and not to look for explanations in relationships outside the group or in the past.

The ways in which these groups use the here-and-now experience to confront feelings can be demonstrated by contrasting how anger is handled in conventional group therapy with the way it is handled in the new groups. If a participant in a conventional group says he feels angry about something, he usually is asked to try and talk about it in more detail; group members help him explore his anger in an effort to help shed light on its origins. In the new groups, the same person would be told to act out his angry feelings, to shout and curse, and to then examine the way he subsequently feels. This experience often leads participants to consider whether they have been totally honest with themselves insofar as their emotions are concerned.

Nonverbal exercises, including the use of touch, are attempts to depict human interrelationships in physical terms, the assumption being that body movements reveal what words often hide. By removing the verbal ingredients from the "games people play," these techniques function to bring important interpersonal issues into focus. In *Milling*, an exercise often used in initial meetings, group members are asked to silently move about while exploring each other in whatever way (touching, bumping, eye gazing) they wish for however long they desire. Deprived of the customary verbal props, "Where do you come from?" "What do you do for a living?" "What do you major in?," members are forced to communicate through other, often more personal, channels. In *Break-in*, another nonverbal technique, all of the members except one intertwine their arms and legs to form a tight circle while the remaining member tries to break his way into the center. This technique is used to accentuate feelings of social isolation, and highlights personal concerns revolving about the topic of acceptance.

Even old fashioned arm wrestling occasionally comes in handy as an effective nonverbal exercise, especially where power, competition, and anger seem to be at issue:

> When the anger takes the form of intensely competitive feelings, along with the surface fear of being defeated which often masks an unconscious fear of winning, the competitive participant may be asked, "Who in this room would you most like to compete with? Or who are you most afraid of competing with?" The therapist may then suggest the nonverbal technique of arm-wrestling, which is quickly picked up by the group and utilized spontaneously as an auxiliary technique thereafter. This involves the competitors placing their two right arms together on the floor or on a table, elbow to elbow, and each attempting to force down the arm of the other. Nearly always, both competitors become intensely involved in it, and as yet the defeated competitor has never seemed to experience any resentment. Usually there is a mutual sense of exhilaration which spreads to the group. Often there are sudden, spontaneous insights as to the meaning of competition. ("I wanted to win, but God, I think I threw the match. My God, am I afraid of winning?") ("It scared me to beat him.") ("I felt as if I'd die if I couldn't win. Didn't know how set I'd be on winning.") (Mintz, 1967, p. 68)

Techniques of this sort, although they sometimes take on the aura of fun and games, are regarded in deadly earnest by group participants. Both confrontation techniques and nonverbal exercises often precipitate profound reactions and have, in some instances, led to severe withdrawal or depression. Many people are not ready to be confronted with material they are unable to assimilate. Accordingly, questions have recently been raised regarding the training and ethical practices of persons who lead these groups.

One serious issue concerns the lack of follow-up services for group participants. Many leaders travel from city to city conducting groups and are not committed to members once the group has ended. In most conventional treatment groups, the therapist remains in the community after the group has concluded and is able to offer help or to act as a referral source if necessary. The new groups, because of their short term nature, usually do not provide this type of back up. A group member who begins to experience severe psychological difficulties is therefore forced to fend for himself.

Those involved in the new group movement counter such criticism by claiming that the new groups are not meant to treat disturbed people but are designed solely for personal growth and are best considered "therapy for normals." This form of psychological elitism, however, is difficult to justify. Where does one draw the line between normality and neurosis, or distinguish between a potential member's tendency to become deeply morose and his potential for serious depression? In any case, there is very little effort by leaders of the new groups to screen out those participants for whom such an experience might be damaging.

Perhaps a more serious criticism of these groups is that many of the leaders, called "trainers" and "facilitators," do not have professional credentials. This is not to say that possession of a Ph.D. or an M.D. is an automatic guarantee of competence. But it does assure that the holder has gone through some form of professional training, one that usually includes years of intensive supervision. Many facilitators and trainers have little if any experience working with human beings; some take on the role of leader merely on the basis of having been participants in a group themselves.

It should be pointed out in fairness that Esalen and NTL both have their own training programs and regularly conduct workshops for professionals in the field. But since group leaders are not accredited or certified in any formal way, anyone can bestow the title of trainer or facilitator upon himself and set up shop with very little background or training. The American public, with its peculiar propensity for quick and simple solutions to complex problems, makes such endeavors profitable and prestigious. After all, what can one lose by being in an Encounter group for a few evenings or for a weekend? The answer is simply that we do not know. Perhaps all that can be said is that if there is something to be gained, there probably also is something to be lost.

Despite the problems associated with the new groups, they seem to be having a positive influence on the more traditional forms of group therapy. Many therapists have begun to seriously consider the ways in which body expression can be used to further therapeutic goals and some have already incorporated encounter techniques into their group practice. Sensitivity groups have been used in the professional training of psychologists and psychiatrists as well as in community mental health projects involving the training of paraprofessionals.

### THE COMMUNITY APPROACH

It is obvious that radical changes are taking place in the treatment of abnormal behavior. In this section we follow these changes beyond individual therapy and group therapy, beyond behavior therapy and the new groups, and arrive at *prevention*, a topic that has been articulated most clearly in the area of community mental health.

The concept of prevention can best be illustrated by conceiving of mental illness as a process, a series of stages in which personal problems and crises arise, solutions are attempted (and fail), and deviant behaviors emerge. Most often, mental health workers intervene at the tail end of this process. The major bulk of mental health work, including the paraprofessional activity described in Chapter 4, involves offering services *after* serious disturbance occurs. A preventive emphasis entails intervening at an earlier point, somewhere between the crisis and solution-seeking stage, and offering alternatives to persons under duress. Referred to as *crisis intervention*, this strategy attempts to prevent the onset of symptoms and the development of asocial behavior.

The concept of crisis intervention is based on the observation that crisis situations carry the potential for adaptive learning as well as for the development of deviant behavior. Under stressful circumstances, many people not only rise above adversity but appear to undergo lasting personality change. Even normal development can be seen as a series of personal crises that, when overcome, contribute to personality growth. Gerald Caplan, one of the leading contributors to the community mental health movement, contends that individuals are particularly open and vulnerable during crises and that direct, immediate intervention, if properly timed, can produce permanent changes in behavior (1964). Skilled short term help at the height of a crisis, accordingly, is believed to be more effective than extensive treatment when the situation has cooled.

Putting the concepts of prevention and crisis intervention together with the need to develop community mental health resources, Morton Bard, a psychologist at The City College at The City University of New York, set out to train police officers to deal with family conflicts (1970). This seemingly incongruous combination turns out to be not so unusual when one examines some of the unique aspects of urban life and the details of police work in a large metropolitan city.

In large urban centers, congestion, competition, and feelings of alienation subject both the individual and the family to continual pressure. The problems of family life are accentuated in the ghetto where poverty and feelings of hopelessness combine to produce the frustration that often erupts in violence. And it is the police—the agents of social control—who are inevitably called upon to quell violent family disturbances.

Contrary to what most people think, more of a policeman's time is spent handling family fights and other interpersonal disturbances than in crime control or law enforcement. And intervention of this sort is not without its risks. A recent FBI report indicates that 22 percent of all police killed in the line of duty died responding to complaints of "disturbance," many of which resulted from family disagreements. The statistics on homicides are even more revealing. Of 634 homicides committed in New York City, 35 percent involved family members or close friends. In a study of 672 homicides in Cleveland, it was concluded that "Homicides committed during robberies receive much publicity but do not represent as great a number of killings as do marital discord and quarrels between friends" (Bensing and Schroeder, 1960).

Despite these statistics, police rarely receive training in family dynamics, human relations, or crisis intervention. They are forced to rely on blatant displays of authority or force, and continually place themselves in physical jeopardy. Traditional police tactics suppress rather than resolve family conflicts and further deteriorate police–community relationships. In an effort to uncover new solutions to such problems, Bard designed an experimental project aimed at (1) making police more effective in the ways they handled family disputes, and (2) helping families deal more effectively with problems by offering constructive help in times of crisis.

Bard's project was carried out over a period of two years and encompassed two phases. In the two-month preparatory phase, policemen selected for the project were given intensive exposure to lectures and discussions on psychological motivation and family dynamics. In addition, they participated in laboratory demonstrations of family conflicts enacted by professional actors. The demonstrations consisted of a series of brief plays written without conclusions so that those taking part in them would have to engage in a certain amount of improvisation. Each of the dramatizations began with the professional troupe playing their pre-arranged parts while two officers waited off stage, out of range of what was going on. At a certain point in the action, one usually marked by a pitched battle, the officers were thrust upon the scene and forced to cope with the immediate crisis. Armed with little knowledge of what preceded the flareup and what the family members were like, they were expected to handle the crisis as best they could.

In one of these skits, an actress portraying the wife cowered against a wall as her wife-beating husband, a tall, husky Negro moved threateningly toward her:

> "He's going to hit me, he's going to hit me again," she screamed as the two cops burst on the scene and split, one of them going to the aid of the stricken woman, the other confronting the man.
>
> "Whaddaya doing that for?" the patrolman snarled at the man as he pushed him toward a corner of the improvised stage. "That's no way to treat a woman, that's no way for a man to act. You're no man." With that, the Negro actor, even though he knew it was only a play, reacted angrily and moved toward the advancing patrolman, bellowing, "Who says I'm no man? . . ." (Sullivan, 1968, p. 144)

Immediately afterwards, the participants discussed how they reacted to one another and why. In the above example, the officer who confronted the husband learned that his way of handling the situation—challenging the husband's masculinity—is one of the more common ways policemen get hurt. Through role playing, the officers came to appreciate how even the most well intentioned behavior can backfire to produce exactly the opposite effect. This "learning by doing" was supplemented by sensitivity workshops in which the officers were encouraged to confront their feelings about themselves as police officers and men, as well as their feelings about minority groups.

In the operational phase, lasting the remainder of the two years, the participants put their learning to the test. Although they continued to meet regularly with project consultants, they now were out of the classroom and in the streets. Designated the Family Crisis Intervention Unit (FCIU), they worked in small teams, covering all reports of family disturbance in Manhattan's 30th Precinct, a lower middle class community of approximately 85,000 people in West Harlem. Whenever a family disturbance occurred anywhere in the precinct a FCIU team was promptly dispatched to the scene.

The results of the FCIU's work is best described by a series of anecdotal accounts. In one of these, a FCIU patrolman narrates his experiences:

> "It was up on 145th Street," he said, "and the couple was from the South. We went in there and I could see right off that this guy was tight, very tight. He was a Negro fellow, about 21 or 22 years old, only up in New York six months. She had called the police because of a dispute— a minor thing. But there he was, a little guy, and he was really tense because when we walked in with our uniforms and our sticks, you could see that his earlier associations with police officers must have been very rough.
>
> "You could see the fear in his eyes, the hostility in his face. His fists were clenched, and he was ready to do combat with us. God knows what he would have done if he'd had a gun or a knife. I moved toward the kitchen table and opened my blouse and I told him in a nice quiet way that I wanted to talk to him, but he's still tense and he's still looking at my stick. Well, the stick is under my arm so I hung it up on a nearby chair, purposely, to show there's no intent here. 'Look, I don't need it,' I'm trying to say to this guy, 'I don't need it because you're a nice guy in my eyes. You don't threaten me, so I'm not going to threaten you.' I've got to show this guy that I'm not a bully, a brute, a Nazi or the Fascist he thinks all cops are.
>
> "So he calms down a little. Then I took my hat off and I said, 'Do you mind if I smoke?' And he looks at me funny. And I say, 'I'm a cigar smoker and some people don't like the smell of a cigar in their house, so would you mind if I smoke?' And the guy says, 'Oh sure, sure,' and you could see he was shocked. I felt he saw a human side of us, that I had respect for him and his household.
>
> "Then the guy sat down and he and his wife proceeded to tell us what it was all about. When we explain to her why she's upset, she smiles. 'Yes, yes, yes.' You see, she thinks we're on her side. Then we tell him why he's mad and he smiles. 'Yes, yes, yes.' Now we're on his side. Well, they eventually shake our hands; they were happy and we never had another call from them." (Sullivan, 1968, p. 142)

The experiences of Albert Robertson, an officer with eleven years on the force and a member of the FCIU, are depicted in a similar episode. The case involves a man and his wife who have been hammering away at each other all night long. The wife is the first to approach Robertson as he enters their basement apartment:

"Look what he done to me; he kicked me in the belly. I want him locked up, officer." He says: "Hell, lock her up, too," and holds out his arm to show where his wife has cut him with a kitchen knife. "I'll go as long as she goes, too; otherwise, you got to fight me."

Carefully, with a look of weariness in his round, good natured face, Robertson takes off his blouse and cap, lays his black notebook on the hall table, and sinks slowly into the only comfortable chair in the living room. "What's you folks been drinkin'?" he asks. "Scotch," the glowering, heavy-set man answers. "Sweetheart," Robertson says to the woman, "get me a small drink, will you?" Then he takes off his shoes and rubs his arches and wiggles his toes, and the man gives Robertson the Scotch, but the drink has no ice, so Robertson asks the wife to bring him some.

"By this time," Robertson explains later, "they're so shook up with me sitting in *their* chair, sippin' *their* Scotch (he actually never drank it) that now we can find out what they're really fighting about. Before you know it, I'm part of the family." (Sullivan, 1968, p. 150)

It is obvious that these officers take a different stance from that usually adopted by the police. As a result of their training, FCIU police have learned not to take sides, not to push, and not to threaten to lock up everyone in sight. They rarely draw their guns and often leave their nightsticks in the patrol car. And perhaps most importantly, they are careful not to threaten a man's masculinity or depreciate a woman's femininity.

An important aspect of the FCIU program was evaluation. While anecdotal accounts provide interesting sidelights on the program's operation, statistical comparisons are necessary to gauge its total effectiveness. One significant finding concerned "pre" and "post" homicide rates in the 30th Precinct. Although family homicides increased somewhat over the course of the study, none of these occurred in the 962 families seen by the FCIU. In addition, no injuries were sustained by any member of the FCIU during the entire two years, a striking finding considering that police who intervene in family disputes are very likely to be injured. By most measures, the experiment was a remarkable success, thus pointing the way for future projects of this sort.

## Conclusion

The various psychotherapies and other intervention techniques reviewed in this chapter represent only a small sample of the many methods utilized to treat abnormal behavior. At the very least, our survey tends to suggest that significant changes are taking place. Even though statistics are not available, there appears to be a discernible shift away from individual therapy and toward the use of groups and the community as treatment modes. This perhaps is understandable if we consider that the types of problems created by a rapidly changing society make social forms of treatment very appealing.

The potpourri of different treatment techniques added to the wide variety of psychological disorders generates a number of intriguing questions. Can schizophrenics, for example, benefit from group treatment? Do neurotics require the services of a highly trained specialist? What is the best treatment for sociopaths? Should everyone receive treatment? All these questions perhaps can be summarized within two basic questions that will confront students of abnormal behavior in the future: Who is to be treated and by what method? Who will provide the treatment?

An attempt was made to answer the first question in the earlier part of this chapter by contrasting the intrapsychic and behavioristic approaches. We speculated at that time that the behavioristic techniques might best handle those disturbances in which symptoms can be clearly identified, while the intrapsychic approaches might deal best with disturbances involving alienation, depression, and feelings of inferiority. We also indicated that certain action-oriented techniques, such as directive therapy, might cope more effectively with schizophrenic disorders than therapies that attempt to enact change through the use of deep emotional involvement and insight. The future may conceivably see a taxonomy of treatment techniques developed such that specific methods may be dictated for specific disorders.

Implicit in the question of what treatment method is best is the assumption that everyone who needs psychological help will receive it. This assumption, as we saw in Chapter 4, is not always warranted. It is an established fact that the majority of persons who are severely disturbed come from the lower socioeconomic classes and are least likely to receive, or be receptive to, traditional forms of psychotherapy. Those who have worked closely with disadvantaged populations point to the deep-seated mistrust in the lower classes toward mental health professionals and their traditional treatment techniques. The economically and educationally disadvantaged tend to be oriented towards immediate concerns and practical issues, and to seek assistance only in times of crisis. Their life values differ markedly from those of most psychotherapists, and consequently they are apt to be shunted aside or treated by quick efficient methods such as drugs.

A growing number of psychologists believe that the only way to cope with the seriousness of this problem is to concentrate on strategies of *prevention* rather than *remediation*. Even if we had the professional personnel to treat all the patients who fill our hospitals, we still do not have the therapeutic technology needed to effectively treat them. Many of the approaches presented in this chapter, although promising, still must be considered experimental. A preventive emphasis would require psychologists to become skilled in developing human resources and to become more actively involved in society's primary institutions. The educational and legal systems as well as the family thus become prime targets for preventive efforts designed to circumvent the development of abnormal bhavior. An example of this was seen in Bard's working with the N. Y. Police Department to create the FCIU.

The issue of *who* will provide treatment was also partially considered in Chapter 4. The feasibility of using paraprofessionals as mental health workers was tested both in Rioch's project involving housewives and in the hospital project utilizing college students. Recent evidence, moreover, indicates that intervention by lay mental health workers is more than just a second-best alternative to professional help. In a recent study, Poser (1966) assessed the effect of group therapy on chronic schizophrenics using professional personnel and untrained college students as therapists. His results clearly indicated that patients in the groups run by college students registered greater gains than those by professionals. The author attributed this to the greater interest, enthusiasm, and energy that the students brought to the situation. These and other findings point to the greater use of paraprofessionals in the future.

Innovative treatment techniques do not occur in a vacuum. Invariably, they reflect changes in the way we *conceive* of deviant behavior. In 1960, Thomas Szasz published a controversial book entitled *The Myth of Mental Illness* in which he proposed that the concept of mental illness functions merely as a social tranquilizer, as a "myth" that tends to obscure certain unalterable facts of life. One is that social living is *inherently* fraught with difficulties. Human beings, he suggested, are constantly faced with "problems in living," some of which lead to the development of behavior that is not readily comprehensible. To suggest that such behavior is caused by some unseen force called "mental illness" only clouds the issue by imposing a disease model upon problems that are essentially social in nature. Perhaps what we are witnessing today is the growth of a "problems in living" perspective and the development of new ways of looking at deviant behavior.

In the beginning pages of this book, we proposed that the methods adopted to treat abnormal behavior are tied to the models of psychopathology that are currently in favor. The foregoing discussion tends to suggest that the models to which people currently subscribe may be undergoing transformations. The intrapsychic and behavioristic models of psychopathology and the talk of symptoms and childhood disturbances appear to be yielding to a more contemporary and socially oriented view of human behavior. Although man's social nature and his need for affiliation have been noted in the past, the model of the future may place increasing emphasis on the interdependency that binds people together. Concepts such as intimacy, reciprocity, and commitment may eventually replace such concepts as the super-ego, fixation, neurosis, and psychosis. Perhaps the model of the future will even include the concept of—love.

# References

---

ABELSON, H., COHEN, R., HEATON, E., and SUDER, C. 1970. Public attitudes toward and experience with erotic materials. *Technical reports of the Commission on Obscenity and Pornography*, vol. 6. Washington, D.C.: U.S. Government Printing Office.

*Action for Mental Health.* 1961. New York: Wiley. Science Editions.

AMERICAN PSYCHIATRIC ASSOCIATION. 1968. *Diagnostic and statistical manual of mental disorders.* (2d ed. DSM–II). Washington: American Psychiatric Association.

ANON. (E. THELMAR) 1932a. *The maniac.* London: Watts.

ANON. 1932b. *I lost my memory: The case as the patient saw it.* London: Faber & Faber Ltd.

BARD, M. 1970. *Training police as specialists in family crisis intervention.* U.S. Department of Justice document PR 70–1 (Law Enforcement Assistance Administration). Washington, D.C.: U.S. Government Printing Office (May, 1970).

BATESON, G., JACKSON, D. D., HALEY, J., and WEAKLAND, J. H. 1956. Toward a theory of schizophrenia. *Behavioral Science* 1:251–64.

BECKER, W. C. 1959. The process-reactive distinction: A key to the problem of schizophrenia. *Journal of Nervous & Mental Disease* 129: 442–49.

BELKNAP, I. 1956. *Human problems of a state mental hospital.* New York: McGraw–Hill.

BELL, J. E. 1961. *Family group therapy*. Public Health Monograph No. 64. Washington, D.C.: U.S. Government Printing Office.

BENSING, R. C., and SCHROEDER, O. 1960. *Homicide in an urban community*. Springfield, Ill.: Charles C Thomas.

BEN-VENISTE, R. 1970. Pornography and sex crime—the Danish experience. *Technical reports of the Commission on Obscenity and Pornography*, vol. 7. Washington, D.C.: U.S. Government Printing Office.

BERR, C. S. 1916. Obsessions of normal minds. *Journal of Abnormal Psychology* 11: 19–22.

BIEBER, I., *et al*. 1962. *Homosexuality: a psychoanalytic study*. New York: Basic Books.

BREUER, J., and FRUED, S. 1950. *Studies in hysteria*. Boston: Beacon Press. (Originally published in 1895.)

BROEN, W. E., and STORMS, L. H. 1966. Lawful disorganization: The process underlying a schizophrenic syndrome. *Psychological Review* 73: 265–79.

BRUNER, J. S. and C. C. GOODMAN. 1947. Value and need as organizing factors in perception. *Journal of Abnormal and Social Psychology* 42: 33–44.

CAMERON, N., and MARGARET, A. 1951. *Behavior pathology*. Boston: Houghton Mifflin.

CAPLAN, G. 1964. *Principles of preventive psychiatry*. New York: Basic Books.

CASHDAN, S. 1966. Delusional thinking and the induction process in schizophrenia. *Journal of Consulting Psychology* 30(3), 207–12.

CHAPMAN, L. J., and TAYLOR, J. A. 1957. Breadth of deviate concepts used by schizophrenics. *Journal of Abnormal and Social Psychology* 54: 118–23.

CHURCH, J. 1961. *Language and the discovery of reality*. New York: Random House.

CLECKLEY, H. M. 1948. Antisocial Personalities. In *An introduction to clinical psychology*, ed. L. A. Pennington and I. A. Berg. New York: The Ronald Press Co.

CUSTANCE, J. 1952. *Wisdom, madness, and folly*. New York: Pellegrini and Cudahy.

DOLLARD, J., AND MILLER, N. E. 1950. *Personality and psychotherapy*. New York: McGraw-Hill.

DRAGUNS, J. G. 1963. Responses to cognitive and perceptual ambiguity in chronic and acute schizophrenics. *Journal of Abnormal and Social Psychology* 66: 24–30.

EPSTEIN, S. 1953. Overinclusive thinking in a schizophrenic and a control group. *Journal of Consulting Psychology* 17: 384–88.

ESQUIROL, J. E. D. *(n.d.) Maladies mentales*, cited in Zilboorg, G. and Henry, G.W. 1941. *A history of medical psychology*, N.Y.: Norton, p. 570.

FARINA, A. 1960. Patterns of role dominance and conflict in parents of schizophrenic patients. *Journal of Abnormal and Social Psychology* 61 (No. 1): 31–38.

————, and RING, K. 1965. The influence of perceived mental illness on interpersonal relations. *Journal of Abnormal Psychology* 70: 47–51.

FARIS, R. E. L., and DUNHAM, H. W. 1939. *Mental disorders in urban areas.* Chicago: University of Chicago Press.

FORT, J. 1969. *The pleasure seekers: The drug crisis, youth and society.* Indianapolis: Bobbs-Merrill; reprinted by Grove Press.

GARMEZY, N.; CLARKE, A. R.; and STOCKNER, C. 1961. Child rearing attitudes of mothers and fathers as reported by schizophrenic and normal patients. *Journal of Abnormal and Social Psychology* 63: 176–82.

GOFFMAN, E. 1961. *Asylums.* New York: Doubleday–Anchor.

————. 1963. *Stigma.* Englewood Cliffs, N.J.: Prentice-Hall.

HALEY, J. 1963. *Strategies of psychotherapy.* New York: Grune & Stratton.

HARPER, R. A. 1959. *Psychoanalysis and psychotherapy.* Englewood Cliffs, N.J.: Prentice-Hall.

HARRIS, J. G., JR. 1957. Size estimation of pictures as a function of thematic content for schizophrenic and normal subjects. *Journal of Personality* 25: 651–71.

HERRON, W. G. 1962. The process-reactive classification of schizophrenia. *Psychological Bulletin* 59: 329–43.

HESS, J. H., and THOMAS, T. E. 1963. Incompetency to stand trial: procedures, results, and problems. *American Journal of Psychiatry* 119: 713–20.

HOLLINGSHEAD, A. B., and REDLICH, F. C. 1958. *Social class and mental illness.* New York: Wiley.

HOLZBERG, J. D., KNAPP, R. H., and TURNER, J. L. 1967. College students as companions to the mentally ill. In *Emergent approaches to mental health problems*, eds. E. L. Cowen, E. A. Gardner, and M. Zax. New York: Appleton-Century-Crofts, chap. 6.

HOOKER, E. 1957. The adjustment of the male overt homosexual. *Journal of Projective Techniques* 21: 18–31.

HUMPHREYS, L. 1970. *Tearoom trade: Impersonal sex in public places.* Chicago: Aldine-Atherton.

KALLMAN, F. J. 1946. The genetic theory of schizophrenia. *American Journal of Psychiatry* 103: 309–22.

————. 1953. *Heredity in health and mental disorder.* N.Y.: Norton.

KATZ, S. 1953. My twelve hours as mad man. *Maclean's Magazine* (Toronto), October 1.

KETY, S.S. 1959. Biochemical theories of schizophrenia: Part I. *Science* 129: 1528–32.

KUTNER, L. 1962. The illusion of due process in commitment proceedings. *Northwestern University Law Review* 57: 383–99.

LANCET, EDITORS OF. 1952. Disabilities and how to live with them. London: *Lancet.*

LEONARD, W. E. 1927. *The locomotive god.* New York: The Century Company.

LEZNOFF, M., and WESTLEY, W. A. 1956. The homosexual community. *Social Problems* (The Society for the Study of Social Problems) 3(No. 4), 257–63.

LOVAAS, O. I., 1967. Behavior therapy approach to treatment of childhood schizophrenia. In *Minnesota Symposium on Child Development*, ed. J. Hill. Minneapolis: Univ. of Minnesota Press.

————; SCHAFFER, B.; and SIMMONS, J. Q. 1965. Experimental studies in childhood schizophrenia: Building social behaviors using electric shock. *Journal of Experimental Research in Personality* 1: 99–109.

MCREYNOLDS, P.; COLLINS, B.; and ACKER, M. 1964. Delusional thinking and cognitive organization in schizophrenia. *Journal of Abnormal and Social Psychology* 69: 210–12.

MARK, J. A. 1953. The attitudes of the mothers of male schizophrenics toward child behavior. *Journal of Abnormal and Social Psychology* 48(No. 2): 185–89.

MEEHL, P. 1962. Schizotaxia, schizotypy, schizophrenia. *American Psychologist* 17: 827–38.

MINTZ, E. E. 1967. Time-extended marathon groups. *Psychotherapy: Theory, Research and Practice* 4(No. 2): 65–70.

MOONEY, C. M., and FERGUSON, G. A. 1951. A new closure test. *Canadian Journal of Psychology* 5: 129–33.

MULLAN, H., and ROSENBAUM, M. 1962. *Group psychotherapy.* New York: Free Press.

NUNNALLY, J. C. 1961. *Popular conceptions of mental health.* New York: Holt, Rinehart & Winston.

O'BRIEN, B. 1958. *Operators and things.* Cambridge: Arlington.

OSGOOD, C. E.; SUCI, G. J.; *and* TANNENBAUM, P. H. 1957. *The measurement of meaning.* Urbana, Ill.: University of Illinois Press.

PETERS, F. 1949. *The world next door.* New York: Farrar, Straus.

POSER, E. G. 1966. The effect of therapist training on group therapeutic outcome. *Journal of Consulting Psychology* 30: 283–89.

RAYMOND, E., ed. 1946. *The autobiography of David* ————. London: A. P. Watt & Son.

REID, E. C., 1910. Autopsychology of the manic-depressive. *Journal of Nervous and Mental Disease* 37: 606–20.

*Report of the Commission on Obscenity and Pornography.* 1970. Washington, D.C.: U.S. Government Printing Office; reprinted by Bantam Books.

RIOCH, M. J. 1967. Pilot projects in training mental health counselors. In *Emergent approaches to mental health problems*, eds. E. L. Cowen, E. A. Gardner, and M. Zax. New York: Appleton-Century-Crofts, chap. 7.

ROBACK, A. A. 1961. *History of psychology and psychiatry.* New York: Philosophical Library.

ROBBINS, R. H. 1959. *The encyclopedia of witchcraft and demonology.* New York: Crown Publishers.

ROKEACH, M. 1964. *The three Christs of Ypsilanti.* New York: Alfred A. Knopf, (Vintage Books).

ROSS, B., and ABRAMSON, M. 1957. *No man stands alone.* Philadelphia: J. B. Lippincott.

SCHEFF, T. J. 1964. Social conditions for rationality: How urban and rural courts deal with the mentally ill. *American Behavioral Scientist* 7: 21–27.

SPECK, R. V. 1967. Psychotherapy of the social network of a schizophrenic family. *Family Process* 6: 208–14.

STANTON, A. H., and SCHWARTZ, M. S. 1954. *The mental hospital.* New York: Basic Books.

STRAUS, E. 1938. "Ein Beitrag sur Pathologie der Zwangsercheinungen," cited in Landis, C. and Mettler, F. A. 1964. *Varieties of psychopathological experience.* N.Y.: Holt, Rinehart, & Winston, p. 339.

SULLIVAN, R. 1968. Violence, like charity, begins at home. *New York Times Magazine,* 24 November 1968.

SZASZ, T. S. 1961. *The myth of mental illness.* New York: Hoeber-Harper.

————. 1963. *Law, liberty, and psychiatry.* New York: Macmillan.

THIGPEN, C. H., and CLECKLEY, H. M. 1957. *The three faces of Eve.* New York: McGraw-Hill.

WATZLAWICK, P., BEAVIN, J. H., and JACKSON, D. D. 1967. *Pragmatics of human communication.* New York: Norton.

WILDEBLOOD, P. 1959. *Against the law.* New York: Julian Messner.

WING, J. K. 1962. Institutionalism in mental hospitals. *British Journal of Social and Clinical Psychology* 1: 38–51.

WOLBERG, L. R. 1954. *The technique of psychotherapy.* New York: Grune & Stratton.

ZAX, M., and STRICKER, G. 1963. *Patterns of psychopathology.* New York: Macmillan.

ZILBOORG, G., and HENRY, G. W. 1941. *A history of medical psychology.* New York: Norton.

# Index